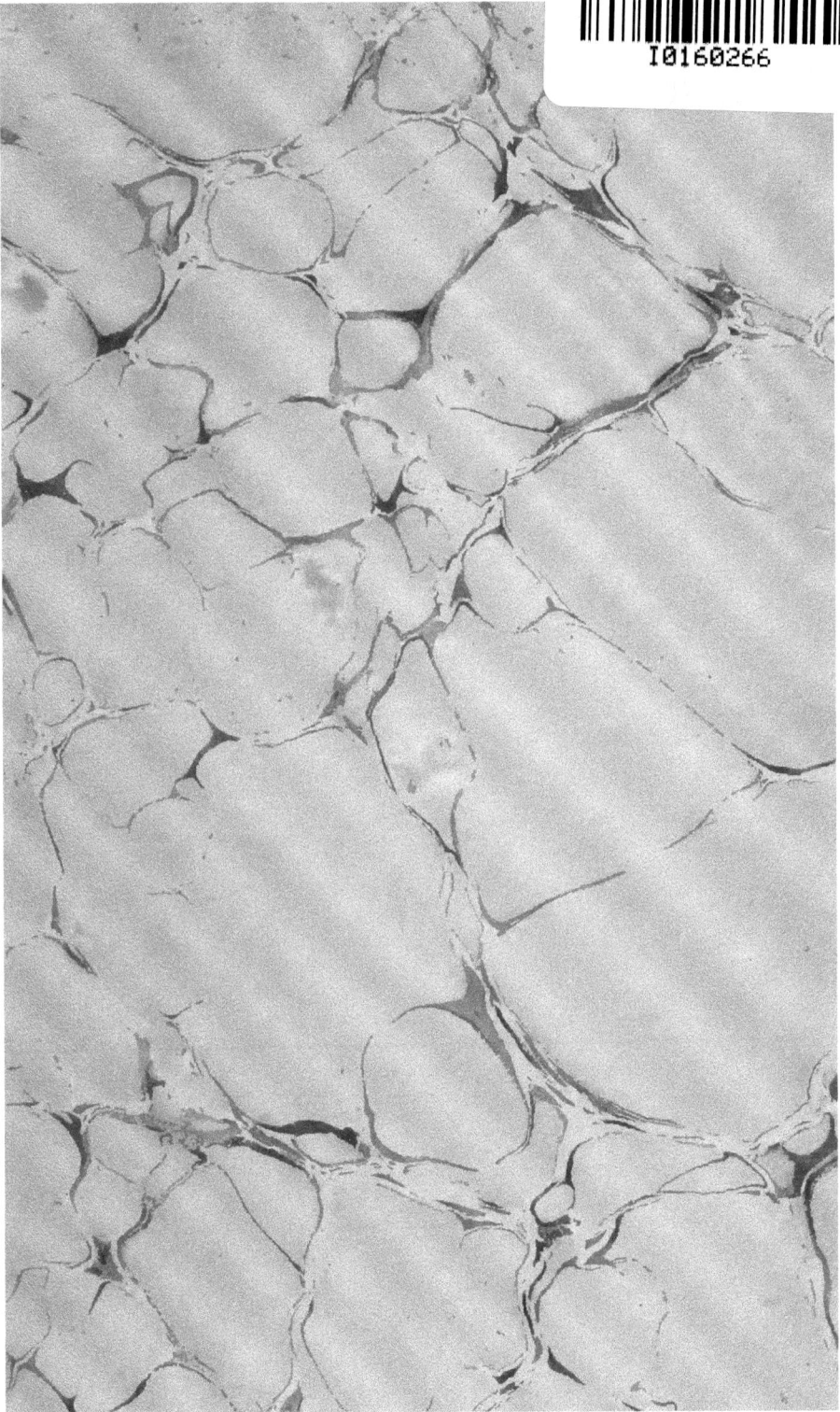

POEMS FROM PROVIDENCE

by BRETT RUTHERFORD

20th ANNIVERSARY EDITION

Illustrated by

PIETER VANDERBECK

THE POET'S PRESS
Pittsburgh, PA

This edition includes updated notes, and revised versions of "Son of
Dracula," "Godmakers," "Avoiding the Muse," "Creation Revisited,"
"Water Sprite," "Indian Rock Shelter," "At the Coke Ovens," "The
Cemetery by the Lake," "Ganymede," "The Ransom of Ganymede,"
"The Turk's Mausoleum," "Sacrifice," "Night Walker," "Night Shift,"
"Trysting Place," "Midsummer Night," and "Mill Towns."
The six poems in the section titled *Midnight on Benefit Street*
are new in this edition.

Some of the poems in this book originally appeared in
*The Newport Review, Haunts, Lovecraft Studies, Crypt of Cthulhu,
Weird Tales, Der Golem, Home Planet News, Liberty, The Brown Classical
Journal, The Moorish Science Monitor, Beyond, Midnight Graffiti,
The East Side Monthly* (Providence), *Chrysalis* and *Ganymede* (U.K.),
and in the limited-edition chapbooks,
*Prometheus on Fifth Avenue,
Thunderpuss: In Memoriam,*
and *At Lovecraft's Grave.*

ISBN 0-922558-58-2 (print edition)
Also published as PDF and wide-format PDF.
Publication date: August 15, 2011
Second Edition

THE POET'S PRESS
2209 Murray Ave #3/ Pittsburgh PA 15217
www.poetspress.org

CONTENTS

AUTUMN POEMS

POEMS FROM PROVIDENCE

THE GOD'S EYE: A SUMMER DIARY

POEMS OF ANTIQUITY

THINGS SEEN IN GRAVEYARDS

ILLUSTRATIONS by Pieter Vanderbeck:

POEMS
FROM
PROVIDENCE

AUTUMN POEMS
1985-1988

OCTOBER IS COMING!

Listen! There is a sudden pause
between my words and the surrounding
silences: no breeze, no hum
of street lamps, no tread of tire —
even the birds have missed a beat.
It is the first self-conscious tinge
of maple leaf red, the first
night-chill of the season.
It is the caesura of equinox —
it whispers a prophecy:
October is coming.

It will not be like any other October.
You will be torn from the things that bind you.
You will follow a strange wind northward.
You will tread the edge of glaciers
   and blush with the iron tinge of destiny.
You will come to earth in a strange place
where you will be known as a leaf
                  from an alien tree
      and be feared for it,
where you will seek the tongue-touch of another
      rasping exile — and find it.

Not for you the comfort of old trees,
      old branches, old roots —
now at last the buoyant freedom
                  of the nearly weightless,
the eyrie-view above pine-tops, eddied above
      rain troughs and lightning rods,
bird-free,

<13>

drifting ghostlike and invisible
         on graveyard mound,
grazing the cheeks of grievers, pausing
     upon the naked backs of lovers,
tracing the mysterious barricades between
     the kingdoms of strays,
colliding with children in their chaotic play —
Hearing at night with brittle ears the plaintive sea,
     the wearing away of shoreline,
the woeful throb of the requiem of whales,
the madrigal of feeding gulls, the thrust beat
     of the albatross in its pinioned flight,
the hideous slurring of squids,
the inexorable gnashing of the machinery
                         of sharks —
Mute, passive, dumb as a dead leaf
     you shall hear them all —

You shall move among the avalanche of first snow,
amazed at the shattering of perfect ice,
its joyous crystalline tone as it falls,
the utterly new dimension of its remaining,
endlessly crushed and compacted and moved,
singed to a fog and sublimed away
as if it had never been, while you
still lay like an old coat in a hamper —
grayer, crisper, more decrepit than ever.

And you suspect your lingering immortality —
a leaf, a brittle parchment that no one can read,
a shard, a skeleton of cellulose,
a thread, a string, a lichen roost, a bird-nest lining,
a witness of ever-advancing decay and assimilation,
by becoming nothing, becoming everything.

<14>

2
Yet this is such an insubstantial fate.
I can think of it now in the context
    of this human frame,
hands to write it, lips to speak it
    as transcendental prophecy.
Not only the dead but the living
can pass to this realm beyond matter.
All who have lived or ever will are there already
but only one in a thousand suspects it.

Why, then, do I crave for touching,
for arm-enfolding tenderness on winter nights?
Why do I ache for the line of a slender neck,
a moist surrender, the firmness of flesh,
the drumbeat sonnet of another's heart
loud in my ears, the harmony
of pacing my breath to another's breath,

falling limbs entwined into a trusting sleep,
or waking first and thanking the gods
for this wall of life between me and uncertainty?

I do not know, except that love
is the fluid of the Muses,
the enhancer of meaning, chariot of purpose,
that one plus one is not two
    but infinity,

that entropy, this modern malaise
    of the wasting leaf
is the false side of the coin of nature —
base metal welded to hidden gold.

<15>

3

Listen! *October is coming!*
It will not be like any other October.
You will be torn from your ease and comfort
by the one who loves you. You will follow
a strange wind northward, not as surrender
to an autumn urge, but as a warrior
for Spring. Glaciers will shudder back
at the green fringe of your beard. Your smile
will make strangers trust you, ask to know
what manner of tree sends youthful emigrants —
even the dry-leaf exiles will stir at your arrival.
You shall not pass the winter in random flight,
    nor cling to the steeples and chimneytops.

Not for you the graveyard and its lying testaments,
not for you the vicarious touching of lovers and losers —

All shall know you and say of you:
Here is the one who loves and risks all.

<16>

You shall not heed the devious sea
and the night-call of Neptune's ravenous hosts.
The owl, the raven, the whippoorwill,
    the squirrel, the cat, the sparrow
shall teach you the ways of their defiance of season,
their hidden thrust for continuance.

Boisterous, active, strident as a new tree
    you shall take root again,
defying the shadow master of winter,
    the devil of frost,
refusing to yield one leaf to the ache-long nights.

And you rejoice in your numbered mortality,
in love, at risk of happiness for a single embrace,
at risk of loss and denial, too —
but knowing it and caring not.

A love, an eye, a heart, a hand,
a witness to ever advancing hope,
one to the power of infinity —
one plus a fraction, approaching,
but never reaching, duality.

4
Which shall it be? This orient autumn
or this renascent spring? This painless slide
into the lush oblivion of ash, or wingbeat
in Daedalus flight to a promised star?

I only know that October is coming.
It will not be like any other October.

<17>

THE STATE VERSUS AUTUMN

RESOLVED: For the sake of decency
and the order of the land,
the Congress hereby abolishes
the unwanted month of October...
No more Octobers ever?
Has the Society to Outlaw Gloom at last
succeeded in the Senate halls?
Has the Lobby Against Dead Leaves
banished arborial pollution?
Resolved: That the falling of leaves
disrupts the conduct of business,
distracts our children from their studies,
depresses the widowed and elderly...
We hereby outlaw deciduous trees.
How long, then, till the squad cars come
with their phalanx of armored cops,
handcuffing my corner sycamore,
chainsawing the neighbor's rowan tree,
tearing the vagrant maple from the street,
screaming with bullhorns for the ailanthus
to disperse from hillsides and parking lots,
interrogating runaway saplings all night,
wresting confessions from an effeminate birch?
The casualties will mount beyond reckoning,
the loss of leaves beyond count,
numbers too large for a superchip
or the chambered cranium of a C.P.A.
It's a conspiracy, of course:
the Moral Majority, the Vatican,
Jehovah's Witnesses, the Mormons,
an arm-in-arm league of Fundamentalists,
their hidden object a simple one:

<18>

Outlaw Halloween! They claim
the day is a Communist plot,
a pact of Satan and Hollywood,
Beelzebub and Publisher's Row.
A turning of innocent youth from God,
an anarchist's field day,
a sadist's orgy of pin-filled apples
and candies injected with LSD.
On Halloween, the faithful complain,
you cannot tell who the homosexuals are.
On Halloween, too much of the world
tilts to the literal Devil's side.

The bill has amendments, of course.
It will be a felony to serve up Poe
to those of tender and gullible age.
Horror books and movies? Goodness, no!
Bradbury's tales, and Brahms' autumnal tones,
LeFanu and Bierce, Blackwood and James,
Hawthorne and Derleth, Leiber and Bloch,
a whole amendment proscribing Stephen King,
real or pseudonymous, and prison for life
for reading Lovecraft and his protégés!

And so, a stitch in time is made.
September's harvest blinks
      to winter's barren hills.
A month of mail will never be delivered.
Today a marshal comes up to my desk,
tears page after page from my calendar.
Someone is blacking out words in the library books.
The date of my birth no longer exists.
These politicians mean business!

<19>

NOT YEARS ENOUGH

How many autumns more? I cannot guess.
How slowly thirteen moons go rolling by,
how achingly the thirty dozen days
count off the torn inked sheets of calendar.
Life wrinkles silently, by phases imperceptible
the skull and bones show through the flesh.
More than the other signs of passing
the shelf of unread books accuses me —
not years enough to read them all!
And all those books unwritten, languages
to learn the lilt of, music to shape
beneath the independent fingers —
millions of words and thousands of melodies.

No matter what, the end must come
before the final page is writ, the coda sung.
Composers dreaded to start their Ninth
of symphonies, but trembled all the more
when the Ninth was done, behind them.

<20>

How many symphonies would they eke out
before the unrelenting knock of Fate?

If only Sleep, that dark-eyed panda,
were less the brazen thief — if only dreams
could quicken the long drear nights
with more than a passing vision.

I do not need to dream-quest Mt. Yaanek —
a quiet study would do, a reading lamp,
a chair and a sturdy book. My *ka*,
my lazy double, my astral body
can lounge on a hammock with a Dickens novel,
or browse through the night-locked Athenaeum.
Never too late to learn the names of trees,
of sleeping birds and withered flowers.

Or maybe I'd walk with book in hand
barefoot in graveyard, a midnight reader
of horror tales, epic reciter.

I'd make the dead listen to the *Faerie Queene*,
count on their fingers the knights and Moors
of the endless *Orlando Furioso*,
wear them out with the embracing lists,
the straw that stuffs the *Song of Myself.*
Maybe my eyes would retrace Shakespeare.

But this is Autumn: lamp-dousing time
for my waking self, long nights sliding
to the gravity of solstice, dead leaves
like pages escaping me unreadable.
Not years enough to read them all,
not years enough to count them!

<21>

THE SAILOR AND
THE OAK NYMPHS

Oak with its roots in core of iron,
lava-tipped fingers reaching to magma,
ancient beyond the reckoning of sun,
brown as the acorn egg that bore her,
branches tightened, taut as muscles
boles a gnarl of screaming faces
   echoes of strange births
    and even stranger lovers.

Her skin bears scars:
  the nettling name of some boy,
the pen-knifed initials of lovers
who long ago subsumed
    into the blur of humus,
the signature of a deeper attack,
knife-thrust of a drunken sailor
who slashed at her one moon-mad night,
breaking through bark to cambium.

She was a long time healing,
but years before the gashes stitched
to spiderlines

they found the man in a nearby wood
   anonymous cadaver
   throat slit by self
   or by an unknown hand.

Knowing this oak,
I know how he came to be there,
I need but taste the tannin
of my October cup, but close
my eyes to see the tale unravel:

<22>

First came the virgin girl,
the gentle Amaltheia,
the tender one who lured him
before the tavern door,
offered him kisses, promised
to walk with him
in the slanted light of the forest.

He waited not far from the bleeding oak.
The fair one broke her promise.
He cursed her, wished for the warmth
　of the familiar dives,
　the hot wet swallow
　of burning whiskey.

And then a lusty nymph appeared,
red-lipped in leather,
a slut who said her name was Io.
Io was inexhaustible
fulfilling his every fantasy,
urging, then teasing,

<23>

then turning to mockery
of his all too human manhood.
Failing to please her,
he rolled away from her,
drifted into an angry stupor.

He lay half-dressed,
disheveled, undignified,
not hearing the flight of Io,
the leaf-crunch arrival
    of the barefoot hag,
the autumn crone, oak-born
Adrasteia, the unavoidable.

Before he could rise
from the cold-wet leaf bed,
she leaped on him,
    her bony knees on his shoulders
    breasts dry and pendant
        through tattered nightgown,
    nipples like withered twigs
    hair limp and gray
        and knotted with burrs,
her breath as she kissed him
the scent of apple rot,
the hint of something dead
turned up beneath wet leaves.

Her cracked voice whispered
the song the oak tree taught her:
of the hundred-handed slayers
  who sharpened knives in caves,
of the red-fanged worms
  burrowing up to find him,
of the arctic wind unleashed
  to follow him everywhere
  like a personal iceberg.

<24>

Then she was gone. He lay
beneath a tilted moon,
  a mocking Venus,
dry-mouthed and aching
with the bite of frost.
He found his pockets emptied,
wallet and coins,
greenbacks among the soggy leaves

his pocket knife,
his comb,
his fine-honed shaving razor
  already open
blade gleaming on a blood red banner,
the singing leaf of the oak tree.

<25>

END OF THE WORLD

Not with a trumpet
  but a whisper. No angels
proclaimed the end. Prophets
with sandwich signs
  did not predict it.
No tea-leaf ladies
  or noted astrologers
knew that the end would come
at half-past eight
  in the morning.

It was a Monday,
  (of all days!)
catching them dressed
for their funerals.

Who would have guessed
that this October,
instead of leaves
the *people* turned
and blew away,
that gravity,
the faithful plodder,
would take a holiday?

First some commuters
on a platform in Connecticut
fell straight into a cloudless sky
trying to hook
  to lampposts and poles
with flailing arms.

<27>

Even the oversize stationmaster
was not immune,
hung by his fingertips
to shingled roof,
an upside-down balloon.
His wig fell down,
the rest of him
shot shrieking upwards.

Slumlords in Brooklyn
dropped rent receipts,
clutched hearts and wallets
as they exfoliated,
burst into red and umber explosions
and flapped away.

A Senator stepped down
from his bulletproof limo,
waved to the waiting lobbyist,
  (sweaty with suitcase
   full of hundreds)
only to wither to leaf-brown dust,
crumbling within his overcoat.

Stockbrokers adjusted their power ties,
buttoned their monogrammed blazers,
pushed one another from narrow ledge
falling from Wall Street precipice
into the waiting sky,
printouts and ticker tapes,
class rings and credit cards
feathering back down.

<28>

Bankers turned yellow,
wisped out like willow leaf
from crumpled pin-stripe,
filling the air
with streamers of vomit
as they passed the roof
of the World Trade Center.

The colors were amazing:
black women turned ivory,
white men turned brown and sere,
athletes swelled up
   to fuchsia puffballs,
Chinese unfurled
   to weightless jade umbrellas.

Winds plucked the babies from carriages,
oozed them out of nurseries,
pulled them from delivery rooms,
from the very womb —
gone on the first wind out and upwards.

They filled the stratosphere
darkened the jet stream,
too frail to settle in orbit,
drifting to airless space.

They fell at last into the maw
of the black hole Harvester,
a gibbering god
   who made a bonfire
   of the human host,

<29>

the whirling spiral of skeletons
a rainbow of dead colors
red and yellow and black and brown
   albino and ivory
parched-leaf skins a naked tumble.

The bare earth sighed.
Pigeons took roost in palaces.
Tree roots began
the penetration of concrete.
Rats walked the noonday market.

Wild dogs patrolled
   the shopping malls.
Wind licked at broken panes.
A corporate logo toppled
   from its ziggurat.
Lightning jabbed down
   at the arrogant churches
   abandoned schools
   mansions unoccupied

started a firestorm
a casual fire
as unconcerned
as that unfriendly shrug
that cleaned the planet.

<30>

THE OUTSIDER

Some say that spring
is made for lovers,
summer for marrying.
I do not know
those seasons:
I hastened on
when others mingled,
passed by alone
amid begetting.
I walked the city
for years not touching,
untouched and unafraid.

I am October.
I am conjured
of its red and yellow fever.
I am outlaw to life,
a thief of eyeballs,
citizen of a larger anarchy,
singer of dangerous
truths, peril to normalcy.

Little the world
loves pleases me.
Autumn-mad trees
mean more than palaces,
an austere tomb
more true than a cottage.

I love the earth —
love more
that vast black space
in which it rolls,
a lost marble.

<31>

I am the leaf that burns,
the candle that lights
  its own extinction,
sunset regarding itself,
sunlight spun round
the arc of infinity
until its end
sees its beginning.

I come out of the sea,
  walk sideways,
  write words
between the tide and shore.

I am the shape
  behind the randomness
  of stars,
the dream that fills
  the inkpot of Autumn,

the hooded Outsider
  who frightens you
  and laughs
then makes *you* laugh
at the absurdity of fear.

Will you stay indoors,
hoarding the apple harvest,
warming yourself
by a dead-tree fire?

Or will you join me,
fellow conspirator,
dance me between
the staves of symphonies,

<33>

roll in this new moon
blanket with me,
leaf-haired and cold
and laughing

giving up everything
to inherit all?

I am October.
  I wait at cusp,
  at equinox,
  at crossroads,

the far-off chant
unfettered wind
nowhere contained
    by walls,

the fire-fletched arrows
of burning Orionids,

the shape upon
  the leaf-strewn hill
that calls you
  and extends its hand,

the eyes in shadow
that will not let you sleep.

<34>

SON OF DRACULA

I was the pale boy with spindly arms
   the undernourished bookworm
   dressed in baggy hand-me-downs
   (plaid shirts my father wouldn't wear,
   cut down and sewn by my mother),
old shoes in tatters, squinting all day
for need of glasses that no one would buy.

At nine, at last, they told me
   I could cross the line
to the adult part of the library
those dusty classic shelves
which no one ever seemed to touch.
I raced down the aisles,
   to G for Goethe and *Faust*
      reached up for *Frankenstein*
         at Shelley, Mary
        (not pausing at Percy Bysshe!)

     then trembled at lower S
       to find my most desired,
       most dreamt-of —
Bram Stoker's *Dracula*.

This was the door to years of dreams,
   and waking dreams of dreams.
I lay there nights,
the air from an open window chilling me,

<35>

waiting for the bat,
              the creeping mist,
           the leaping wolf
the caped, lean stranger.

Lulled by the lap of curtains, the false
sharp scuttle of scraping leaves,
I knew the night as the dead must know it,
waiting in caskets, dressed
in clothes that no one living could afford to wear.

The river town of blackened steeples,
    vile taverns and shingled miseries
had no appeal to Dracula. Why would he come
when we could offer no castle,
no Carfax Abbey, no teeming streets
from which to pluck a victim?

My life — it seemed so unimportant then —
lay waiting for its sudden terminus,
its sleep and summoning to an Undead
sundown. How grand it would have been
to rise as the adopted son of Dracula!

I saw it all:
how no one would come to my grave
to see my casket covered with loam.
My mother and her loutish husband
would drink the day away at the Moose Club;
my brother would sell my books
    to buy new baseball cards;
my teachers' minds slate clean
    forgetting me as they forgot all
    who passed beneath and out their teaching.
No one would hear the summoning
    as my new father called me:
Nosferatu! Arise! Arise! Nosferatu!

<36>

And I would rise,
    slide out of soil
        like a snake from its hollow.
He would touch my torn throat.
The wound would vanish.
He would teach me the art of flight,
the rules of the hunt
    the secret of survival.

I would not linger
    in this town for long.
One friend, perhaps,
    I'd make into a pale companion,
another my slave, to serve my daytime needs
(guarding my coffin,
    disposing of blood-drained bodies) —
as for the rest
of this forsaken hive of humankind,
I wouldn't deign to drink its blood,
    the dregs of Europe

We would move on
    to the cities.
The pale aristocrat and his thin son
    attending the Opera, the Symphony,
    mingling at Charity Balls,
Robin to his Batman,
    cape shadowing cape,
    fang for fang his equal soon
        at choosing whose life
            deserved abbreviation.
A fine house we'd have
    a private crypt below
        the best marbles
            the finest silk, mahogany, brass
            for the coffin fittings
Our Undead mansion above
    filled to the brim with books and music...

<37>

I waited, I waited —
   He never arrived.

At fifteen, I had a night-long nosebleed,
as though my Undead half had bitten me,
drinking from within. I woke in white
of hospital bed, my veins refreshed
with the hot blood of strangers.

Tombstones gleamed across the hill,
lit up all night in hellish red
from the never-sleeping iron furnaces.
Leaves danced before the wardroom windows,
blew out and up to a vampire moon.

I watched it turn from copper to crimson,
      its bloating fall to treeline,
      its deliberate feeding
   on corpuscles of oak and maple,
      one baleful eye unblinking.

A nurse brought in a tiny radio.
One hour a night of symphony
was all the beauty this city could endure —
I held it close my ear, heard Berlioz'
Fantastic Symphony: the gallows march,
the artist's Undead resurrection
amid the Witches' Sabbath —
my resurrection. I asked for paper.
The pen leaped forth and suddenly I knew
that I had been transformed.
I was a being of Night, I was Undead
since all around me were Unalive.

<38>

I saw what they could not see,
walked realms of night and solitude
where law and rule and custom crumbled.
I would feed on Beauty for blood,
  I would make wings of words,
      I would shun the Cross of complacency.
A cape would trail behind me always.
I was a poet.

<39>

THE ARGUMENT

"Two decades ago that scribbler Poe — "
Longfellow smiled and took tea,
" — that *jingle writer* as Emerson dubbed him,
called us but frogs 'round the Common,
likened our poems to croaking.
Well, he's dead, and I'm writing still,
and that's an end to it."
His auditors nodded, some heavy-eyed,
as the old master recited *Evangeline*.

<40>

One sunny day, quite unintending,
I find the old bard's tomb in Mt. Auburn:
a grassy knoll well-fringed with yews,
a stately monument, the letters
L O N G F E L L O W
immense enough for all to read.

But whom should I discover there,
perversely lingering, casting their shadows
upon the stone that weighs the poet's brow?
Whom but a trio of stately Ravens,
borne on their wings from an unknown shore,
rebutting the greybeard poet's boast,
ending the argument — forevermore!

<41>

AVOIDING THE MUSE

Silent this voice for more than a year now —
homeward I come again with head bowed down,
weighted with other laurels and their debts,
back to poetry and its finer lyre.
Time and this book alone shall tell if I
am any wiser than I was before,
or if the Muse whose hardened gaze I dodged
shall reconcile herself once more to me,
come to the window I deck as of old
with that dim flame that She and no other
can see. Heartbeat pentameters return,
furrows I plow anew; bones, rock & root
I move away, to plant a newer crop:
trees that will rise to the bellies of clouds,
roots tapped in the strata of dinosaurs,
leaf sprouts that will themselves contain whole books.
From one thought, many lines; from but one dream,
a vision framed at the heart of epic;
from sap of imagination, the sword
of heroes and the gods who inspire them
to plant a Troy, a Rome, a bright Asgard,
as hope against the all-devouring night.
Shield-maiden of Bard, Skald and Poet,
Muse, take me back! Have I not given up
everything to make these lines? Look at me,
Muse: the fading wraith I am, you made me.

<42>

ASHES AND EQUINOX,
MARS IN CONJUNCTION

In Memoriam Barbara A. Holland[1]
September 21, 1988

1
What manner of wind brings news of you —
of your last talon snatch at life —
but a fitting one, a hot ash current,
the burnt-pyre smells of Yellowstone
hustled by schizophrenic winds to choke us.
For days the soot flakes peppered us.
Again and again we lifted the pen
to ask someone, *What's burning?*

Who could have guessed that Adrasteia
(she whom the shivering Greeks
    named *Unavoidable*)
took up the cudgel from her cousin Mars,
ran down the tinder slopes with torch,
tossing hot coals from her tresses,

or that she'd tramp the parched plains eastward,
stirring up tempests in the Mexican Gulf,
riding some Greyhound in bag-lady pride,
bearing your death in a tight brown bundle,
timing her storm-drop to the very equinox.

Earth shakes, sloughs off a life.
  Pale threads of you ride up
      to join the auroras,
  a boreal ripple like wind
  in the nap of your raccoon coat.

---

[1] Poet Barbara A. Holland died in New York City on the equinox of 1988, with
planet Mars in its closest conjunction in many decades, while fires raging in
Yellowstone filled Manhattan's skies with eye-scalding ashes. Talk about omens!

<43>

The clouds make way,
open a blue door with a streak of cirrus.
Something in space, some presence as vast
and drear as a forgotten god,
as real as that bond between things
and the words which distinguish them,
something shudders in welcome and joy,
sings to its brethren, *A poet is coming!*

2
Even Mars leans jealously near,
hoping for one last chance to catch her.
They need a Sibyl and a female bard,
word-knitter to ever-shifting beats.
Chanting they watch the earth star's orbit,

thirst in their salt-sand necropolis,
not for a transfer of water or warmth,
a trout or an apple or a flying cow.
No, Mars needs poets, too!
Let her come as her final years revealed her,
purblind and limping and ragged,
shield-maiden to the last, welcome
so long as she comes with *words* on her tongue!
They watch the flare of coronal light
burn from New York into stratosphere.
They hold webbed hands and watch the meteor,
tektite incarnate with olivine eyes. They wait in vain:
she leaps through Martian air in overshot
toward the all-embracing arms of Jupiter.

(She called him Wotan, Wanderer,
    cries out as she sees his great red eye,
        his overweening gravity.
His captive moons sing out in chorus
    At last, at last — a poet is coming!)

<44>

3
Yet these are only words and whimsies.
Nothing goes up. Nothing continues.
Animate defies inanimate
year after year and then a day too many.
We are left with clay like any other clay.
And yet, like earth,
                with its million secret gemstones,
these fragile leaves are crystallized thought.
The words remain. The poems are children
locked in a Gorgon glance in their perfect moment.
Life ends. It is such a brittle thing,
brain walking on vein and synapse
tight-roped over nothingness.
                                    Yet mind and hand
conspire against mortality,
make life a book relived again
at every reader's humor.

4
A poet is dead. How then
can this city have a hundred turnings
where I still hear her lines, re-see her seeings:
my fire escape once woven with tentacles —
that warehouse transformed to Venetian palace —
the garbage can upon whose lip
the limp banana lily languished —
the Village streets astride with crutches
    and flying fish —
the whimsies spun
                from Magritte canvases —
If there be gates to a life unending
the only ones I know are books.
Open the covers! Turn the pages!
Sing out, Listen! *A poet is coming!*

<45>

WRITER'S BLOCK

For Barbara A. Holland

This object is clearly out of hand:
just when the charcoal monolith
popped up in the gutter
  like fungus
is not so important as how
it grew at curbside,
consuming a parking space,
  a bus stop,
cracking the plexiglas shelter
until the smooth black slab
  jostled a tree
  and warped the sidewalk,
flush to the bottom step
of your brownstone front!

It festered there,
  absorbing sunlight
  like a vampire bat,
its height advancing
  in bamboo stealth
to the edge of your curtains,
an anxious bird perch
that finally shot
  to rooftop.

Your morning view is night, now —
starless black basalt
without a hint of aurora.
Your darkened rooms
hunch in resentment.
The potted palm
  yellows and dries,
your windowsill
  a hecatomb of withered flowers.

<46>

And all the while
   your typewriter jams,
   pens clog,
as a parallel mountain
   of crumpled paper
   accumulates.
Poems germinate
   in bean sprout lines,
but the stanzas coagulate
   into thought-clot,
abandoned verse
   as useless as
   a castaway scab.

<47>

This state of things
  will never do!
If the Mayor refuses
  to move the impediment,
I know a consulting shaman
adept at elementals.
He will circle your house
with Indian maize
(to the delight of pigeons),
hang silver spoons
on your mantel.
Then he will pull the tail
  of the Wendigo,
enraging his northern eminence
until its four crossed winds,
its burning feet of fire
converge at the pinch point,
galeing down Hudson,
huffing from the piers
to your doorstep,
pounding that monolith
flat as a paving stone.

He has done this for others —
that is why,
  at certain corners,
dust devils harry pedestrians
on windless days,
tornado leaves and paper scraps,
raise skirts and strip
the skins of frail umbrellas.

<48>

The shaman's fee
    and these lingering vectors
of anarchic wind
are but a small price to pay,
lady, a paltry ransom
for imprisoned sunlight,
fettered typing,
    and a hostage pen.

One way or another,
we will set you free.

<49>

BOARD GAME

It is a game that never ends.
No one returns to the place where he started.
All the players are mad — and terrified.
They never cease to throw the dice.
They close their eyes and
                go through the motions,
yet no one has ever taken the prize.
One plays with the cool eye of a tactician;
another believes in magic; a third
insists the gods ordained everything.

The madness is when you fall in love.
The terror is when another player
loves you. The deck is loaded,
the laws of probability lockset
against the overlap of lusts.
The pile of gold has never been seized.

<50>

The loved ones lay helter-skelter,
unclaimed, their tokens aligned
like seraphim on shards of a shattered
frieze. Face down, the good luck cards
are never upturned and revealed.

Each player is madly in love;
each player is madly pursued.
No one ever lands on a square
where the object of his passion
awaits him. (With brazen leaps
the chessmen elude you; with haste
you flee the hateful embrace
of your relentless lover.)

Thus the dice roll,
the cards deceive,
the wheel of fortune
spins, the god
of chaos laughs.

Any number may play.
The rules change constantly.
No one uses his real name.
Everyone goes home alone.

<51>

CREATION REVISITED

1

According to Ussher,
the Bishop chronologer,
the act of Creation commenced
no later than Four Thousand
and Four
Before Christ —
thus spake the annals
of the *knews* and *begats*
traced back to *Genesis*.
Those Hebrew midwives
remembered everything!

According to Lightfoot,
an even more accurate Anglican,
God started the commotion
on Sunday the 23rd
October, 4004 B.C.,
fossils and Darwin
notwithstanding,
to the very morning,
to the very hour
of God's day shift
a workmanlike 9 AM.

2

Now just imagine
the confusion of Adam,
wandering through jungle,
surveying the plains,
leaping to hilltops,
alone on the Eighth Day,

his God mysteriously absent
after the sudden, tiring burst
of creation: Man, the afterthought.

<52>

He finds himself alone,
lord and progenitor,
mouthing the names
of leafed and feathered things,
saplings and hatchlings,
chrysalis and cub and lamb —
big-headed and knock-kneed
lnone knowing their names,
their natures,
ignorant of who should eat whom,
oblivious to sex.

Adam revels in the chaos,
in his sole possession of
the magic power of naming.

But now the horizon rages
with whirlwind, flashes
with fire-tongues, shakes
with terrible thundering.
A heaven-arching demon
splits the zenith, its eye

<53>

reptilian, its formless
cloud-bag hung with tentacles,
an airborne jellyfish.
Its vacuum maw extinguishes
unwary birds, uprooting
trees, reaching for Adam.
Its suckers engulf him,
lift him to cloud-top.

And Adam screams, eyes shut
at thought of too many eyes
and countless tentacles. No way
to make a name for this one!
He weeps at the thought
of his own annihilation.

God laughs, resuming his form,
the gentle greybeard Father,
puts Adam on mountain peak,
roaring with merriment
at the first man's terror.
Leaves him mystified
to clamber back to the garden,
asking *Why?*
against the unanswerable.

First day of his life,
he is seized by a monster,
mocked by his Creator.
Last day of October.
Halloween, 4004 B.C.
Trick or Treat.

<54>

DEER HUNTERS

for Don Washburn

1

The Berkshires, pre-dawn, in dead of winter.
This is a ghost of a forest: trees skeletal,
their bark a parchment of wrinkles and agony,
scarred by birds and the mange of moss,
their brittle fingers intertwined, the ropes
of grapevines knotting in strangled wedlock.
They cannot swat the squirrels, shrug
the nests, or shake the beehive away —
like hungry in-laws they are here to stay.
Pines drag the soiled skirts of boughs,
needles darkened to widow's hues,
around them a circle of colorless humus,
    bleached moss and needles
    snake skin and spoor of owl.
Amid the brush and orphan saplings
the ground is a scavenged battlefield:
the exploded hand grenades of pine cones;
spent shells — the hollow vesicles of berries;
crashed planes — the crippled wings of seedpods;
suspicious mine — a collapsed and wrinkled apple;
barbed wire — the windblown line of barbs and burrs;
dead soldiers — a frozen marching line of mushrooms,
helmets askew and fringed with ice.

This is a ghost of a winter. Where is the snow?
Surely these brittle gems of frost, these daggers
of ice rainbowing the cold colossus of sun,
these random patches of white cannot be all?
Where is the snow? What drove the birds away
and stripped the color and raiment of leaves
from these chattering and groaning trees?

<55>

Is it invisible, this imago of Winter?
Has it come impotent and snowless,
huffing cold air to frighten us,
looting the passive oaks and maples as a mugger,
limping along with pines as crutches,
freezing the soil with its name,
like the armies of Tamerlane,
    Alexander and Bonaparte,
before whom cities threw open their gates?

The cold is real, the snow — imaginary.
The past is dark and barren as heartwood.
Beneath the peat and clay it echoes blizzards,
the hunger of wolf for the thinning herds,
forgotten bones of saber-toothed banquets,
dream-racked hominids with hatchets of stone,
the agonized slide of a glacier,
the earth-shake cry of the birthing of mountains —
surrendered to a winter that will not show its face.

The false sun, orange, impossibly huge,
does not even wink at the imposture.
It forms a leaded rosette window
behind the lattice of elms,
the twist of willows, the white slats
of upright birch. A shallow stream
collides with a night-chilled pond
(fish press against its frozen sky
until the surface disintegrates.)
A rabbit watches the ice mosaic dissolve.
A woodpecker taps defiance.
Then silently, like courtiers in silken robes
in some incensed and muffled palace,
the deer emerge from laurel thickets.

<56>

Brown earth to tawny fur, scant snow
to bob of white tail, branch tangle
to the rack of spreading antlers.
It is time to move, to follow
the oldest buck's imperium.
They turn toward the sleeping town.

2

North Adams Inn
They smell of beer and tobacco,
gunpowder and sweat. They grunt
and eye the sleepy waitress

<57>

(the fathers knowingly, in jest,
the sons emphatically, in earnest).
The kitchen blinks on at 4 a.m.,
the dining room chilled
   from a wind-shattered pane,
their breathing billowed,
hands warming at the fill of cups
with brain-quickening coffee.
The signs hung everywhere
say *DEER HUNTERS WELCOME.*

So why did a midnight howler
rip panes from their sleeping rooms,
blow dry Arctic winds
      in their blankets,
topple their guns, shells scattered
         across the carpet?

One boy — his first hunt — lay stark awake
as the picture window sheared off,
torn from his fevered erotic dream
of a brown-skinned girl with the eyes of a doe.
The clear night stars arrested him,
pulled him with stellar gravity to room edge.
Winds lapped his face. He cried out, horrified,
as he saw who strode the mountaintop —
the hunter, the giant, implacable Orion.

Numbly he crawled to the womb of blankets.
He dreamt of the rifle his father gave him,
of stalking the deer in a pinball forest
      of death and blood and brimstone,
      of lifeless doe eyes accusing him.

<58>

The men and boys don their
flannel coats, their fur-
lined caps, lace up their boots,
check pockets for matches and shells,
    the silver flask of whiskey,
    the knife, the map, the compass.
They cram into the big-tire pickups,
roar off toward the mountains.

3
        The Deer
The town is comatose. It is the wolf watch,
the turning time before sun-up, too soon
for clatter of milk and bakery trucks,
too cold for anyone to be about
to see the single-file march of the deer,
their stately parade down Church Street,
hoof-clattering echoes as they turn down Main,
their antlers a spindly Burnham Wood,
their eyes and muzzles surreal in streetlight.
They pause to glance in the dark shop windows,
white tails wagging in puzzlement
at the show of useless merchandise.
They file into the hotel, the waiting lobby.
The signs have been changed. Now they read:
    DEER WELCOME.
Baskets of apples have been prepared for them.
Some sleep till noon in their cozy rooms.
Others watch game shows and situation comedies.
Hooves dance behind DO NOT DISTURB placards.
Yearlings order exotic salads and apple cobblers,
view rock and porno videos with astonishment,
Bucks sharpen their racks on mahogany bedsteads.
Fawns flush the toilets and run in terror.

<59>

The does take bubble baths.
At dusk they burst through the lobby again,
startling the guests and chambermaids,
bolt up side street to a vacant lot,
herding to woods at wolf-chase speed,
following the stream bed upward
to the brown palace of primal forest.

The downcast hunters return in silence,
the fathers morose, the sons resentful,
their manhood blood unproven
as if past hunts had been empty lies.

<60>

GHOSTS

Ask ghosts if there's a Heaven
or if they linger here to haunt
because the lips of Hell
fire-tongue the fringe
of their continuance.

Why need to loiter
in chill old mansions,
in potter's fields,
dank woods and fens,
in crenellated ruins,
if Paradise tugs
at the gowns of the dead?

Ask any ghost if he
would rather be alive!

<61>

ECLIPSE

How like the moon, that sullen wanderer,
to brush between the earth and sunlight,
how rude to cast her shadow here,
a breath of cosmic space to mar
the warbling afternoon with shivers!
New England conceals itself in clouds
like an embarrassed spinster.
Street lights blink on in Boston;
shoppers and businessmen
walk hushed in their wolverine shadows.

<62>

The moon rolls on, its icy pall
relents, the spotted sun disc
glares above cloud-banks, trumpets
its triumph in unseen rainbows —
bouquets of rose and vermilion,
violet and gold, banding the earth.
In gardens and planters and empty lots
the tendrils of clinging vines obey
their ancient diurnal clockwork.
The soft blue horns of morning glories
open confounded to the falling sun.

<63>

EDGAR AND HELEN

Edgar Allan Poe and Sarah Helen Whitman, 1848
An Imaginary Romance

1
They walk the sunlit avenue, the parasol
concealing her face as she says,
                              "How grand
you have come all this distance to see me."
She wears a dress imported from France,
confounds him with a haughty roseate scent.
"I will not permit you, of course,
to fall in love with me."
                              He grips
the black valise. His hands turn white
as sheaves of poems fall out
beneath the feet of Sunday crowds.
"Alas," he says, retrieving them,
searching her eyes as she stoops to help,
"If such were possible, then —
Then it is already *too late*."

By chance she finds the poem
    inscribed to her:
I saw thee once — once only

She reads it and averts her gaze,
pretending to favor a floral display.
The suitor knows he has pleased her.

In the strange rooming house he broods
as unrelenting opiates of memory
draw moonlight *houris* in Helen's form.

<64>

He thinks of how he can win her,
sway her will with his eloquence,
his life and poems at her feet,
merge with her gentle bookish life,
take her back to his humble cottage
or *stay* in this love-charmed Providence.
He dreams of the thousand ways he will love her.

<65>

2

Moon and the flames of candled glass
conceal her features but reflect his tears,
his wild-eyed deafness to her final refusal.
                              "Friend always
will I be, in the chastest manner. No more,
yet no less than a sister can I be to you."
He rages at the insults of Helen's mother —
(how Helen were better dead than married
to a godless drinker of the Plutonian lees) —
chills at the echo of her sister's chatter,
the gossips and slanderers anonymous,
who wrote the warning letters to Helen —
damn them all who would thwart his happiness!

She wears her heavy cloak against the cold,
on top of that a black, superfluous shawl,
as if to italicize her widowhood.
                              "I love you,
Helen, as I have never loved before.
Our poems speak the truths you would deny."

"Do not torment me with vows of love — "

"You torment *me*," he stabs, "with beauty,
with scintilant brilliance of eye and mind,
with promises a suitor cannot mistake,
nor chaste propinquity requite."
He takes her frail, cool hand, cups it in his.

Her profile is cold as Athena, her eyes
turned inward in agony, in thought
of the aged mother, the invalid sister,
the imminence of her uncertain health,
the wisp of wine exhaled
    from the trembling suitor's breath.

<66>

"Neither by word nor glance, nor yet by deed,"
she answers him, withdrawing her palm
from the heat of his impetuous grasp,
"must you ever show that you love me.
I cannot be torn from my place and time.
We are poets. Our words have loved,
but we are separately doomed to solitude.
I cannot bear your loving glances."

<67>

3
Coffined in his sleepless rooms,
he poisons himself with laudanum.
He thinks of the thousand ways he will kill her.
He sees her ravaged on a riverbank,
imprints on her breasts of a legion of rapists.
He sends a gibbering orangutan
to stuff her corpse up the nearest chimney.
He bricks her in with her poetry.
He puts her mother beneath the pendulum
(the more she talks, the faster it falls).
He sets her sister adrift on a raft,
circling the Maelstrom ominously.
A raven persists on her window ledge.
The Red Death sweeps down Benefit Street.

At vision's height he dresses and walks
the darkened brick alleys of Providence.
He climbs the steep hill to her corner,
spies the darkened windows above.
He will stand here till dawn,
deceived by the rustle of curtain,
the imagined flickerings of candles,
the creak of floorboards and stairs,
the glint of moonlight on brass.

The clean sunrise will banish him,
burning away his ardent love,
    his ineffectual revenge,
leaving him an empty vessel again,
drifting from this friendless seaport,
south, to court a darker mistress,
a veiled widow who refuses no one,
and whom no one ever leaves.

<68>

VISA GRANTED, WITH GRAVEL

Enough
    polite letters to the Ministry
Enough
    waiting for the refusal of visas
Enough
    bread-dry mornings for the good of the state
Nothing
    will stand between him and freedom
Nothing
    but the wall that entombs Berlin from the sun
Nothing
    but a little barbed wire, a
    handful of guards with tiny bullets,
    the frown on the face of the portrait of Lenin
Nothing
    but a guardhouse pin-pocked
    with bullet holes, dusty macadam
    rust-stained with fugitive blood
Nothing
    but gravity prevents him from leaping over
    but inertia prevents him from charging through
    but brick and stone —

If the wall is an immovable object,
he must become an irresistible force.
One truck
    cargo his girlfriend
    his eight-month-old child

One truck
    piled high with proletarian gravel
    seven tons weighted to the limit
    all but the needed gas siphoned away
      to prevent explosion
    turned into a high-speed ram to test
    Newton's laws against the state's

<69>

One truck
>hurtling toward gates like a reckoning
>outspeeding the reflex to aim and shoot
>breaking through wood at Checkpoint Charlie
>breaking through bricks at Checkpoint Charlie
>breaking through concrete for the dream of —

The astonished guards fire at the juggernaut —
>one shoots to miss and thinks *Lucky bastard*
>one shoots to kill because no one
>>should escape the People's Paradise

A hundred miles of brickwork tremble
as the seven ton passport crashes through.
Another hairline crack mars the perfect wall.
The East shrugs and transfers
>the files of two workers
to the black cabinet marked *Former Persons*.
Though someone else will have his room, her place
at the University, friends repeat their names
with reverence, as though a transcendent world
had lifted them into the clouds like saints.

It is this:
A letter to the editor. A report to the Western press.
A polite petition. A week in the anteroom
of the Ministry of Refusals. A guest suite
in the Hospital for Maladjusted Workers.
Or this:
A truck with smashed headlights
>and a crumbled hood.
A load of gravel. Eye to eye
>with captors and guards,
foot to the floorboard at last *doing something*
weeping at coming out alive, shouting for joy

breathing the free air on the other side of the wall

<70>

BORDER GUARD

Now and then, a man whose job it is to shoot
his fellow citizens, enjoys a day at leisure.
He does not go to a crowded cafe. The dreary
bleached faces on television annoy him.
The films and books he would like to see
are forbidden, the satire plays closed down.
He walks down streets that have forgotten
their names, opens a twisted gate and walks
into a ruined cemetery. He likes it here.
These people died before the bombs,
    before the chapel became a shell,
      when the living had time to honor the dead,
        the patience of stone carvers
          to mark their passing —
      when the living had space to house them
        each in an individual grave —
not the quick, anonymous flame of cremation
      nudged from behind by the next in line.
The trees were planted before he was born.
    No one nails slogans to them.

<71>

These crows are not informers.

A shard of stained glass falls to the ground:
a saint's eye, a halo chip, a puzzle
piece of a forgotten benediction.
An acorn descends, a leaf
tears away from the structured tree.

Why should one leaf among its classless brethren
defy the order and symmetry of oakdom
to make its assuredly fatal plunge?

The acorn must fall,
the squirrel must do his duty
and bury it. Even a new oak
that springs unintended from its sepulcher
is doomed, each tree
another jailhouse, a jabbering asylum
under an iron sky.

But a leaf — a leaf has a chance —
a wind might catch it, a bird
might seize it from an updraft
and carry it to freedom.
Who knows what becomes of one *over there?*
Maybe an anarchy of leaves, maybe
a touch-me-not defiance of order,
maybe they plant themselves
                    on any tree they please —
oak and ash and willow and holly,
the plane and the pine,
a jostle of maple and cedar and birch —
melting pot trees in a jigsaw forest —
or maybe a peaceful wood, each uniform tree
striving its best toward the eternal light? —

<72>

Why should one man, fed and provided for,
his job assured, his humble bed, his state-
assured cremation — why should one man
cry *nay* against the law-compelling land,
to burst through the checkpoint
                    where *he* was trained
to shoot at any outlaw breakout, to stop
the spy, the saboteur, the secretor of wealth?
He thinks of the truck that barreled through,
of the joy and terror on the driver's face,
how he had fired to miss, thinking *Lucky bastard*,
how his comrades had failed to stop the seven

ton juggernaut, how no one really wanted to.
He knows of dozens of failed escapes, knows
the bloodstains, the bullet holes, the patches
in the length of the hundred mile wall.
On the other side there are wreaths for those
who died trying. "Did them a favor,"
the sergeant boasts. "What would they do
in the decadent West anyway? Nothing but drugs
and poverty. Nothing but trouble."

Next day, the sun beats down accusingly,
a fusion-powered torchlight, soul-baring.
He walks to his station like a criminal,
fears the secret police could read his thoughts,
like banners hung from a dirigible.
He takes his rifle and rounds,
his heavy coat and helmet, assumes his place.
His stern reflection in the guard-post glass
fools no one — he is a frightened boy:
tired of this game, these dullard playmates,
this oppressive school. He drops the gun,
slides out of coat and helmet, turns with
a voice not quite his own and says to the guard

<73>

beside him, "Comrade, what if I crossed
the checkpoint now — what if I walked
right into the West — would you shoot me?"
His companion's face locks in agony.

"You didn't say that, comrade. I didn't see you.
My gun — " he smiles — "My gun could jam."
He waves to the guards on the other side.
He takes a breath. He runs,
and no one fires a shot behind him.

Where an oak leaf trembled and fell
a piece of sky now admits the blue
of the alter heavens. The leaves are astir.
They don red jackets for their breakaway.

Where once a guard stood resolute,
a question mark settles like a gull,
a dare replaces a salute.
The guards are all investigated.
The sergeant who assigned the guards is demoted.
The lieutenant in charge of the sector
is brought before a loyalty board.
The army considers more robots and dogs.
Along the wall, the stones themselves
shift in their mortared places and ask
Why are we here?

<74>

GODMAKERS

I, Moishe, who by the sweat of my beard
these tablets carved, have been alone for weeks
with wind on mountaintop, a quarrier,
stonecutter, and, as I learned at Thebes,
inscriber of laws for the silent god.
No one speaks to me; not even thunder
can tap the *shalts* and *shalt nots*
on flat-face basalt: it is my sense
that tells me a decalogue, a single god,
a unity instead of the carnival host of Egypt,
a simple law to lead men to virtue,
a single god to lead them
  to a time beyond all gods,
the age when every man is Moishe.

One day a better one shall climb
this lifeless crag, summon the gods,
and one by one the hoary ones,
yea, even *Yahweh*, will gather here.
Upon the bloody plain of Canaan
the gods shall justify their ways
to man, and man shall judge them.

<75>

And then he will send them away,
down to the long sleep of history,
saying, "Go now, ye gods; you were
the playthings of our growing years.
Once you became a mask that hid us
from our better selves, then we forgot
that rag-doll wishes cannot truly live.
The lie that sired you, made us kill,
rape and enslave our neighbors. In god's
name we slaughtered the makers of gods.
Answer, Yahweh, for the anxious servitude
of Jewry; Allah, for your wild-eyed
prophets; Brahma, for your dung-fly poverty;
Christ, for your born-again monsters,
loving to hate, and hating to love.
Answer, and then go off and die."

<76>

SIDEWAYS, IN PASSING

Why does seeing you,
  a passing shadow
  peripheral,
your familiar visage
(distracted or likewise
avoiding a direct encounter) —

why does the mere sight of you
leave me in turmoil,
infest my elsewise
  unpeopled dreams,
bring the bile of your name
  to my lips?

Perhaps for the same reason
that *not* seeing you
makes every rounded corner
a stroll into an ambush
of your absences,

makes every evening outing
a boomerang
that circles your lighted windows
before it lets me home again.

<77>

PASSING 17.1.92 PV

You have become an allergy,
an antibody to my peace,
a needle that jabs me
with the impossibility of forgetting,
   the violence of denial,
   the harshness of judgment.

Perhaps we need these shocks,
   these repulsions,
   these double-barreled
      explosions —
they help us recharge
our pact of mutual avoidance.

<78>

VALKYRIES ON ROUTE 128

About those three blondes in a convertible —
a red one that wings on the six-lane thruway,
a blood-red Chevy that seems to leap over
the concrete barriers, weaving the maze
of plastic cones and flares and flashers
without a dent or a mishap. They never
turn off at a cloverleaf or pay a toll.
No one has ever seen them at Ho-Jo's.
Lately they've started arriving at accidents,
pull men and boys from their flaming cars,
drape bone-broken bodies across the hood
(some dead, some moaning in final agony,
all in the prime of their youth and beauty,
death-clenched hands around bottles and cans).
No one knows where they take them.
Tourists see them with their bloody trophies,
hear strains of Wagner doppler by,
yet minutes later they can't be found
by any convergence of patrol car,
roadblock or chopper or radio alert.
CB truck drivers report more sightings
before or after a major collision.
The police are understandably perplexed.

<79>

IVAN GROZNI

Ivan Grozni
Tyrant of the Oprichniks
Little Father to the trembling serfs.
Your murders pale, poor Ivan the Terrible,
beside the deeds of a fat old man —
a pensioned auto worker
          front porch grandpa in old Cleveland
a beer and pretzel neighbor
          picnics and barbecues
          ball games on the radio
nodding to sleep before the television.

He is another Ivan, *Ivan Grozni*,
Ivan the Terrible
          lord of Treblinka
counting the days to his
          Social Security check,
his numbered entitlement —

As Ivan he numbered his subjects —
gypsies and Jews and misfits,
counted them by the hundred,
gassed them by the thousand,
bookkeeping entries at every
          ten thousand mark,
medal from the Führer
          for every tenth
          of a million exterminated,
numbers on a golden arch of death

<80>

Gold watch retirement gift —
good man on the assembly line,
speedy with wrench and rivet —
how many cars did he finish?
A mere few thousand, maybe,
nothing to match
the nine hundred thousand
            he prodded in
            through the one-way door.
He understood efficiency.
            Their slouching gait
            not fast enough,
he whipped and prodded,
maimed and mowed down
the laggards and lame ones.

(His fat hands picked out
            the defective bolts,
dropped them to bin —
never asked where
            they went —

Tried for his crimes
he rallies his wife and family,
hires an attorney to fight
this case of mistaken identity.
He smiles at the battered old Jews
who say they remember him,
call him the Beast of Treblinka,
waves to the courtroom audience
and says in Hebrew —
                        I am innocent.
I am not Ivan the Terrible.

<81>

Yet who are these ghosts
that crowd the air,
clotting the room with accusation?
Who are these legion whisperers,
nine tenths of a million strong
chanting like monks at a Tsar's interment
singing like bells of monotonous iron
one steeple truth in a landscape of lies:

Ivan . . . Ivan. . . Ivan Grozni.

<82>

SPARE CHANGE

Ivy league derelict
begs quarters from students
at the edge of the campus —
annoys professors, shakes down
the bankrolled college boys,
the former President's daughter —

hurtles across street
to meet new quarry
leaving his twine-tied
bundles on the sidewalk.

His chosen place
  is the gusty side
  of the seven-story tower
  (library whose bulk
  wind tunnels the air
  into a frenzy)
where he must button his collar —
an unseasonable place —

<83>

dust devil's playground
when all around is calm,
an arctic stretch
oblivious to time of year.

Is it by accident he lingers here
    or does he sense its chaos,
        its vagrant spirit,
its rushing to meet you
    with a beggarly arrogance?

Does he laugh
    at your torn umbrella
    your wayward skirt
the pages of your thesis
        blown into traffic?

Does he fancy
    these gusts his personal servants,
    hounding and pelting you
    when you refuse
to dip a hand
    into the swollen pocket
    to pay his dues?

The lean troll smiles,
    counts his quarters
    towards a sit-down dinner,
reties the knots
    on his amorphous bundles.

Is he the guardian of gales?
Who knows what hurricanes,
what compressed whirlwinds
  he might unleash
if once those knots untangled?

<84>

WINTER SOLSTICE,
COLLEGE TOWN

Today the sun is a tumor.
It glows behind an eye patch cloud.
The college boys are fleeing town
    long hair   sleek skin
    some purely beautiful
    others already changing
from demigod to semi-brute.
The girls move frigidly
legs torqued as though on skis,
their eyes the neutral shade
    of greenbacks
          home to daddy.

<85>

Black ponds with scum of ice
reflect the withered shrubs,
tent poles of an abandoned circus,
the fabric of summer now skeletal
wind-torn   picked clean
by the talons of desperate birds.

Winter is honest, at least,
the buildings cease being
     a moil of students
exploding in their underwear,
become mere lines and girders,
empty interiors.

Trees rise to meet you starkly
     requiring no deconstruction
     absolutely themselves —
no makeup   no wigs of false curls
     no semiotic cues
     no perfumed bribery
taut arms twisted
     from chase of sun's recession
twigs held tense
swollen with unsuspected spring
blossoms and leaves like library books
logged in, reserved and waiting.

<86>

MILL TOWNS

Old factories:
    how painfully forgotten!
Once, the hopeful immigrants flocked to them.
Workers and foremen built cities around them,
    if not exactly blessing the ground they stood on,
        grateful at least to have escaped the whip
        or starvation where they came from.
The railroads webbed out to meet them,
    branch lines and sidings eager to take
    the crates and bundles from their gates.
Without them
    the towns have forgotten the reason
        of their founding.

What did they make?
    cotton and calico prints,
    steam engines and locomotives
    parts of machines uncountable
    and the tools to make other machines
    and their parts uncountable,
    rope walks, brass foundries,
    lace- and jewelry-making,
    light bulb assembly lines,
    refrigerators and fountain pens,
    and glory! a piano factory —

<87>

all now only names in peeling paint
checkered on bricks and falling signs.

The nearby houses are humbled now
              with torn clapboards,
   rot beneath the stage paint of shingles,
   the cheap bluster of aluminum siding,
   walls bloated, foundations shifted,
   split into rat-cell studios for commuters.

Many are boarded-up, foreclosed.
No one remembers when mansard slate
   and gable and cupola gleamed new,
when a smokestack with a man's name on it
was a place arrived at as a good sign
              of a continued paycheck.

Things that got made here,
   kept getting made.

<88>

Now these sad brick temples accuse us:
    their plywood-covered windows,
    their undecipherable placards,
    the weed trees on their loading docks,
the mystery of abandonment.
Like unburied dead they haunt the roadside,
sombre in daylight, shunned and abhorred
when their shadows grow long at dusk.
They will not burn, their wearing away
protracted by fences and guardians.
(Heirs living on compounded interest
preserve them like Chinese puzzle boxes
they cannot open or understand.)
At night, another commerce lights up
the sidewalks along the chain-link fence
as women sell the only thing they have
from the pavement, and men in cars
circle, circle, hands offering dollars,
other hands offering, and taking, small
envelopes of powders and crystals.

Some midnights, the ghost machines awaken,
their ungreased axles screaming,
drive shafts spinning of their own accord.
A dynamo turns, and furnace mouths flicker
in the cool blue flame of St. Elmo's Fire.
The power looms weave an invisible shroud:
it is long enough to enclose a city.
Tombs without occupants,
they wait for the rites that no one will pronounce.

<89>

PLAGUE

It is a plague —
an epidemic
millions are infected,
never knew they had it.
We must test and quarantine the carriers —
jail for those who spread it willfully.

Ban them from teaching,
from laying hands on children,
from passing it on to others.

Human Intolerance Virus
is caught from ministers,
from Catholic cardinals,
demagogue candidates.
It breeds in repression,
guilt and self-loathing,
spread by casual
  classroom
  locker-room
  barroom chatter.

Millions ashamed of their genitals,
their animal urges,
   their polymorphous nature,
millions insulting the universe
   by worshipping a god
who picks the wings off flies!

<90>

It is time for action —
close down their TV ministries,
bolt up their churches,
put them in special camps,
where they can await their rapturing
without annoying the rest of us.

Hurry along to your god, believers,
   to the one who made you
   in his smiting image!

<91>

JUST REWARDS

WELCOME TO HEVIN
a sign in jagged lettering
nailed to a gap-toothed fence.
Chickens run to and fro on the dirt road.
The smell of manure laces the air.

I must be dreaming.

                        No dream,
comrade   said an expressionless face
behind wire-rimmed glasses. His
hair was tangled, his T-shirt torn,
his words a snarl of sarcasm and garlic.

It looks like a farm. I thought —
                              You thought
Heaven would be a city, comrade?
You're in for a few surprises, then.
Things have changed in the Afterlife.
We angels are into collective farming now.
This sector's exclusively potatoes —
you'll be assigned here, until the end
of the current Five Year Plan.

But I hate potatoes. And I've never gardened.

Of course you hate them. That's why you're here.
Just make your quota for a couple years,
maybe you'll work your way up to fresh fruit —
a little shade there, and no digging —
or maybe a clerk's job later if you're lucky.

*I didn't think it would be like this —
not for me with a Ph.D. and all —
I mean, am I really dead?*

<92>

                              Dead
and buried, buster. You bought it,
as the army guys used to say.

But what's going on here? I was GOOD.
Heaven is reward, not punishment.

OK, fella, let me fill you in on Heaven.
This place used to be a country club, see,
until all the social engineers came along.
The upper classes monopolized God,
Mary threw balls for the Beautiful People,
Jesus and the Saints took care of the poor.
The Arabs and Jews had a bowling league.
The Buddhists chanted, the Hindus built temples.
A lot of people just watched TV and ate,
sometimes four or five generations in a house.

Sounds pretty good to me.

                    Well, see that sign?
It says ALL ARE EQUAL BEFORE GOD.
                    And see this,
it says ALL POWER TO THE PEOPLE.
                    That's the law.

You had a revolution? Here?

You got it, comrade. Now God's a generous guy,
most times you want something, you get it.
It happened when all these Marxists arrived.
They weren't quite bad enough for hell,
those Party cranks and college professors,
and not quite good enough to leave things alone.
They were no sooner dead than they started a Party.
They got Socialists and Fabians,
    Wobblies and Anarchists,
    Leninists and Trotskyites,

<93>

Stalinists and Maoists,
Progressives and Existentialists,
a whole army of semioticians.
Now Lenin and Trotsky and Stalin and Marx
aren't here to encourage all this stuff —
they're in the Other Place shoveling ore.
But all these ink-stained fellows, they formed a
government, turned God out of his temple,
made Him sulk behind Saturn for a while
until He came back and agreed to share power.

So here's the picture of Paradise. No music,
'cept maybe the weekly folk-song rally.
The food is some kind of biscuit, not that
you need to eat — it's just a habit.
On Sunday you get potatoes and cabbage soup.
Everyone wears T-shirts and jeans.
                    Men and women
the same. No one uses his old name.
No one gets to see his family or ancestors —

But my wife must be here ... my mother and father...

Maybe they are, but you're not allowed
                    to find them.
See that poster? FAMILIES PERPETUATE
        CLASS OPPRESSION.
You might see your wife at one of the lectures,
the ones for the politically incorrect like you.
But don't let the Secret Angels see you talk to her.

Secret Angels?
                    Shh — there's one now!
The damn things look like doves, but they're wired.
A Monitor Angel is always listening somewhere.

Are there really angels here? You don't look like one.

<94>

I was made one years ago, but I cut the wings
as a gesture of solidarity with the peasants.
 I want to see God. I want to protest this.
He's just down the road — that place with all
the billboards. Look for an old wrecked Ford
and the painting of Comrade Mary, Mother of God,
riding the cab of a harvester. Can't miss it.

Maybe if enough of us talk to God —

                              Forget it.
His Son's in league with the Communists anyway,
and He gets anything He asks for. But why
complain, man, this is *Heaven*. For all
its faults it's the place where everyone is equal.
In Hell, they make you work for wages.
In Hell, the geniuses and homosexuals
get all the breaks. Someone's always proving
he's better, more talented.
They wear makeup and design fancy clothes.
They build themselves houses
        and tear them down again.
They even have a newspaper called *Hell Today*.
All that foment and striving — no one is ever content
or happy. Man, don't knock it —
this is the People's Paradise!

<95>

THE EVANGELICALS
ARE COMING!

Who needs witchcraft in this hexèd world?
Who needs Sabbats and the weaving of spells,
or an outcast crone to read the runes,
when the goat-horn shadow of the Old Deceiver
hangs over the praying hands of evangelists!
One lays hands on cripples and hypochondriacs.
One reads ailments with the help of a hidden
radio receiver. One lisps that the hated gays
are scourged by God for their unrepented sins.
Another assures us that Jews will never see Heaven.
(Where have we heard these odious lines before?)
Committees of Vigilance invade the schools,
the library flickers with hungry torchlight.
We must not read magazines with nudity,
must not give children books with sex.

<96>

Dungeons and Dragons promotes the supernatural;
these horror films just have to go!

I do not like the dry lips of these accusers.
Their Bibles' leather wrappings snap like whips.
The joy they take in hunting for sin
is a thinly veiled erection, their glory in burning
a wet dream of pyromania.
I do not like their penchant for conspiracies:
the ethical humanists; the homosexuals;
the horned legions of child abductors;
the bearded Elders of Zion with protocols;
the darker races yearning to miscegenate;
every rock guitar an offensive weapon.
They'll stand at the rail in Paradise
(the tickets sold, the places assured),
to watch the rest of us burn in Hell.
They're looking forward to the spectacle.
In fact, they can think about little else.
They even believe in a literal Devil.
They ought to know. They're planning
to run a minor demon for President.

<97>

BLUMENSTÜCKE

The parlor frowned with politeness.
An elegant clock, its walnut rubbed
in the proper grain, ticked quietly,
its pendulum restrained from flight
inside a spotless catafalque of glass.
Nothing was out of place: no dust
could mar the banister, lest white-
gloved hands might intimate
the decline of domestic servitude.

The books, unread and neatly
shelved, stood neck to neck
in regiment, a leather-bound school
of aged and unused nuns.
A golden-threaded tapestry
depicted unicorns at play
in some Arcadian grove
of knotted yews and crags.

The service for six, on trays
that refused to oxidize,
held tea, and a modest supply
of perpendicular sweeteners —
the cups just small enough
to weight the curve of a fragile hand
with no excess of gravity:

weak tea, of a kind to excite
no headiness, brimmed orange
at the spout of an heirloom pot.

The ladies filed in at three,
sat in their places: chairs,
straight-backed with but
a hint of cushioning.
No angle of wood was evident
that might admit a slouch;

<98>

the round piano stool
severely barred duets
at the upright clavier.
A musty book of hymns
and ill-used parlor tunes
(nothing later than Mendelssohn)
was opened to pepper
the eye with dainty arpeggios.

At four, the unsexed minister arrived.
Their talk, as afternoon
expired outside, was of
important things: the times,
the fall of Man from innocence,
the certainty of their
immortal souls.

The flowers paled in nakedness.
Beside the clock, a pistil rubbed
itself and groaned within a
captive marigold. Inside the vase,
concealed by the chaste round dance
of nymphs, and shepherds
who never manage to catch them,
a bee masturbated an iris,
buzzed seductively in roses' ears,
spreading the pollen of everyone
to every female orifice.
The petals quaked in ecstasy,
the stamens stiff to bursting
with overzealous pollen.
The combinations were shocking
as species crossed species.

<99>

All was confusion: the male
    entwining the male,
the females in Sapphic frenzy,
the bee inventing new cravings
as fast as leaf and flower
could furl to them.

The orgy spread to the parlor and beyond.
A cloud of spores surrounded the ferns.
The potted palm uprooted itself.

The willow leaves ached against windows.
The hedges danced and disentangled,
exchanging partners, forgetting
their proper place and station.
(The gardener will be most alarmed!)
Between the bricks of the sidewalk
the sighing moss undulated.

Only the poor drowned tealeaves
seemed unaffected by yearning.
Inert and passive they lay there,
staining the antique porcelain,
submitting to cautious sampling,
to the neglectful cooling
in the lengthy subjunctive clauses
the minister began and abandoned.

"Ah me," he sighed, apologizing.
He dropped a lump of sugar in his cup.
"I fear I've quite forgotten
the subject — what was I speaking of?"

<100>

Just then the pander bee arrived
between one lady's ear and flowered hat,
and so she turned and blurted out,
"Why, we were speaking of penises.
What we were really wondering is
whether in fact you have one,
and if so, how big is it?"
The hostess promptly fainted.

<101>

ROADSIDE VIEWS

It is the way of travelers,
this selective vision,
collective amnesia.
Some look up only
at the sudden blue
of bayshore or green
of an unscathed forest.
I am doomed to the fret
of unremitting vision.
I must sing the song
of rust, tarnish, verdigris,
warehouse and oil tank:

cement trucks immobilized
like a pack of armadillos
behind the high wire
fence, their bellies empty;

lots full of resting buses,
exhausted commuter trains,
cabs battered insane
    limping to junkyard.

Between the towns
we are taught to ignore
the kitchen midden
of technology:

castaway windows and auto doors,
timers and beams and rubble,
dark spans of rusted trestle
fenced off and going nowhere;

<102>

the pointless mud-pies
where tractor and crane
shift earth into the platitude
of parking lots;

the ominous barrows
of dumpster landfills,
black barrels piled high
in cyclopean heaps,
stenciled *Poison*,
their green and iridescent
residue leach-dripping
into incredulous soil.

Cat tails drink oil slick,
    eels burrow away
like a neglected conscience.

Railyards sunstreak
with new forsythia.
Whipsnakes of gold
cry shame on the jaded
commuter, oblivious
to *The Wall Street Journal*,
to the poker game,
to the blurred drunks
in the club car

blooming for joy.

<103>

RUINS

Passing the gutted neighborhood I think of you.
Your soul is that abandoned factory whose panes
lie shattered on its concrete floors.
    The pigeons roost
inside the eaves where keystone
                   — and conscience —
once held the bricks into a nobler form.
A high fence surrounds you needlessly,
braided with thorns. Yet any would-be
trespasser can see the sky clean through
your vacant casements. Unhindered rain
comes through the roof and makes dim lakes
in which your machinery hunches
like islands in an archipelago of rust.
Your doors hang twisted, the locks no longer
deceiving the packs of feral boys
who spray unreadable obscenities
upon the inner lining of your skull.
FAK, they say. *RIGMO WAS HERE.*
VOTE FOR NO ONE.
POST NO BILLS UNDER PENALTY OF LAW.
Rats nest in every orifice. They gnaw at you.
Pink squeals of rodents fill the night.
Your ivy beard is clogged with their commerce,
pack rat bazaar of lint and paper scraps,
urgent memos and bills of lading.

<104>

Today the weathered sign shall fall face down
upon the veined macadam parking lot.
Today the scavengers shall peel your walls
of copper and brass and chrome and wire,
make off in a pickup through a brazen gap
in your fenced perimeter. No one laments
your debasement — like Zion you are stripped
of your jewels by a psychotic god.
I pass you in the southbound train,
remember vaguely how I thought I loved you,
before the empire of your charm collapsed,
before your edifice of seeming fell,
before your calamitous default —
seized for the unpaid taxes of the heart.

<105>

WATER SPRITE

Who made you,
this full moon night of lilacs,
like spring itself aburst,
made you leap from the bulrushes
of park lagoon
bare shoulders wet
from the limpid waters
   your long hair sungold
   bleached white
   in lunary light —

who made your visage
   the sculpted dream
   of surrender
your eyes the blue
   of hyacinth
   of lapus lazuli

who made you run naked
   to greet me
then leap into forest
   of chameleon trees

made your fleeing soundless
   as your bare feet
   sought stealth of moss
as I followed —

made shards of you dissolve
   in dapple of moonlight
   in fall of blossom
   uncurling fern and
   peeping mushroom —

<106>

who made your soft
voice beckon me
leading me deeper in woods
    in circle
coming confounded to a rock
at the other edge of the pool —

made you whisper
as ripples subsided
    from a sinking point:
I am yours: mad angel
    of your destiny.
You will follow me forever.

I will always elude you —
escape to the other surface
    of water
    of mirrors
run through your hands
    like mercury.
I am yours. I am not yours.

Who made you? Who makes me
    follow you?

I walk home slowly, inhale
the languor of cherry,
the braggart bloom of magnolia,
the luxury of lilacs —
who could resist this moon,
this dionysian spring?

<107>

It draws us,
  real and unreal
  mortal and mythical,
quickens the water to form you,
draws your spirit
  to my substance,
my solitude
  to your incompleteness.

Shall I return to find you?
Or shall you seek me out,
coalescing from rainstorm,
pressing through window-screen,
cooling my heat
  with your smooth pale skin,
  the patient ardor of ocean,
the murmur of brooks in my ear,
the taste of dew on your lips,
arms strong as river currents,
the lilac scent of your impossible hair,
the clear blue window
of your eyes above me

<108>

THE GOD'S EYE: A SUMMER DIARY

BLUEBERRIES

Throughout the forest of summer
a harvest of blueberries
ripe for the picking —
memories a decade or more
like good wine aging
(some sweet, some salty
as tears, some acid
with the turn to vinegar).
Like nodes on the neurons
of time these tiny fruit,
deep blue with dusty tinge
of gray and white,
ink blue as the tracings
of faded diaries,
ripening on knee-high bush.
I take your random harvest
from what the birds left,
from what a prior hiker
disdained to pick,
from what another eye
dismissed as not yet ripe.

I take a handful of berries,
eat from my hand,
and at the burst of them
this summer and summers past
wrap round about themselves
the spun yarn in a God's Eye.

<109>

Time is an endless line
wound in a rhomboid orb
so that a yesterday, today,
and certain tomorrows
are parallel. What hand
might strum them, linking
a century, a year,
an instant, a frozen glance
into a single throbbing chord?
Perhaps that is why some things
seem to have happened before,
why certain words and images
vibrate with prophecy.

<110>

INDIAN ROCK SHELTER

Rock shelter at Wanaque,
an overhang of gneiss,
a rainy dusk, a hurried
search for deadwood kindling,
logs for the campfire,
a quest for dry repose.
We sit on the damp ground,
brush off mosquitoes and gnats
just as the Indians did,
pausing at this hidden streambed
to fill their water-bags,
to clean the deer for the journey home,
to sleep uneasily below stone,
fearing its foot-stamp,
the closing of its igneous maw;
watching the scurry of albino spiders,
the view in sputtering firelight
of the drained shells of crickets
webbed in forgotten crevices.
I hear between the cadences
of my own poems and the beat
of my friend's listening,
the choate pulse of rain
on fretted fern, on leaftop
tympani, on roof of rock.

It is here that the stream of our friendship
resumes for a night from diverging
tributaries — one blue, one umber brown,
rejoined, then parted to rivers twain.

When we have told our mutual
tales, skirted the ten-year
mystery of avoidance or silence,
it is the far past that sings to us,
the decade of our broken words
a heartbeat in the life of these stones.

<111>

A shaman sat here, useless for hunting
but dragged along for good luck,
for his spinning of forest epics
of the founding and losing of villages;
for the games he plays with the restless boys.
He has the gift of images:
his agile hand takes charcoal and draws
upon the inner surface of a deerskin –
his cloak and drawing board.
Young boys gather to watch his sketching,
squint in the firelight to recognize
the gods and monsters and animals.
He draws the secret emblems of the hunt.

A tree trunk pierced by a lightning bolt.
   (May the Great Storm pass us by!)
A helpless tortoise turned upside down.
   (Let him who is lame or slow not hinder!)
An arrow in flight with an eagle.
   (Aim straight as the talons of sky-birds!)
A skull bone lost in a barrow of rocks.
   (Keep the hungry dead from our campfire!)
A long-house inside a magic circle.
   (Make our home invisible to enemies!)

The shaman spins tales of the fabled white men,
of a future war and a bounty on scalps.
He does not like this war; he knows
that horsemen with fire-sticks will come,
that his people will become a memory,
a name on the land, confounding the tongues
of the children of strangers. He knows the wood
will bow tame, its herds diminished,
its winter wolfless and snug in cabins.

<112>

He sees the God's Eye prophecy
and looks away. Wiping his deerskin
clean he takes the water pouch, rinses
the bitter ash of face paint. A thin boy —
the next shaman — runs up and fills his palm
with storm-wet berries. He stares
into the quickening heart of the fire:
Smiling. Here, centuries ahead and trembling
as our own fire dims to hearth-glow,
I look right back at him; my thought-forms
tell him this night spins round and round
the rhomboid web of infinity.

<113>

AT THE COKE OVENS

I wanted to see my childhood home again,
the country house, the demon-haunted
rooms that gave my inner self their imprint.
We drove through Scottdale with its too
many churches, stores boarded up, cold
as an exhausted and empty mine.
                        Looking for Carpentertown,
we drove back and forth in the hollow,
passing again and again the barren, black
lot by the edge of the fen. "Stop here,"
I said. "*This* is the place. The house
stood here. Back there, coke ovens blazed
all night, and there, the trucks
ground by with their tons of coal."

Of the house that stood here — nothing.
Of the solemn poplars of Lombardy
        that wrote on my window panes — nothing.
Of the stately porch and its swing,
        the apple tree's promise — nothing.
Of the locked, steep attic and its
        imagined relics — nothing.
Of the deep, deep cellar with its warden rats – nothing.
Of the cool spring house and its poisoned well —
        nothing.
Of the very stone and shape of foundation,
        the lineament of property — nothing.

Am I seeing the future? Is carboned ground
a resonant prophecy of bomb-fall —
is this desolation my past – or a future
of our own time sewn with apocalypse?
(The God's Eye blinks but cannot answer.)

<114>

A neighbor comes to tell us the house
burned to the ground some fifteen years ago.
The timbers and bricks were trucked away.
Slag dumps drifted, quicksand consumed,
until the foundation itself was buried.
Trees tumbled to ruffian winds.
              And as for the "quicksand"
I thought I remembered, the local said:
"Oh yes, out there in the middle,
there are bad places. Last spring it got
our grandma: she was in past her knees
when we heard her screaming and pulled her out."

We walk where the house was,
where it seems dry and safe enough.
Breaking through black-crust earth
the stalks of lichens, brittle, rigid,
stand at attention with lurid caps
of crimson. (The field guide shows them,
and says they are called *British Soldiers*.)
They rise like the whiskers of a Chthonic god,
eyeless guardians of a plain of night,
a carpet for Gorgons and barefoot Maenads,
dry to the touch, coarse as sandstone.
Only their form suggests the organic.

Concealing the lichens, as forest hides shrubs,
I see a tangled maze of blackberries,
thorns guarding the fruit with jealous teeth.
Although they hang at arm's length, ripe
for the taking, although the sickly birds
glare down from a chancred tree, no one
will pick this fruit. It too is black —
coal dust, charcoal, coke and obsidian,
a berry hued for the Stygian shores,
for the lips of the dead and the damned.

<115>

I played here as a child, amid the thorns
And poison ivy. The earth did not open
to swallow me. Perhaps I am immune,
the one, who remembering, belongs.

There is not much left of the great coke industry,
when the coal was eked from nearby Hecla
and the smouldering coke went to Pittsburgh.

A quarter mile back, the red rust scavenges
the twisted wheel of a coal crusher,
its chute and trestle and engine works gone;
it lays like the useless jaw of a dinosaur.
Open hearth ovens sprout vengeful trees,
vine roots split mortar, firebrick moults clay.

"I lived here many years ago," I said —
not saying how many. It was thirty —
I was five when this house protected me,
when its terrors wrote themselves upon me.

And so the hungry past steals up behind me,
a lumbering truck full of fossils,
heating my poems to the red fury of ovens,
erasing my life as quickly as I write it.

<116>

THE OWL

We walk the forest in drizzling rain,
pretending not to mind it, every now
and then wiping water from hair and brow,
conscious of one's earth-and-grass clogged
boots getting heavier by the moment.
Ben strides ahead, proud and happy
to share the peace of his hundred acres,
Hannah beside him, helping to name and observe
the thousand species of shrubs and berries,
the untamed tangle of farmer's woodlot.
The soil is shallow, Ben tells me, so trees
grow only so high until inadequate roots
no longer withstand the leverage of wind —
and so the giants topple and die. And yet
we come upon that stately ash,
its trunk a hundred years or more across,
its leaves like knives or spears defying
the wind next time, the winters yet to come.
There is always one exception to a law.

<117>

Moving to field and orchard, Ben names
the sapling fruit trees, remarks how few
will grow in this stingy-summered North.
Here it is order — next to the female tree
with its bridal blossoms, placed at a kind
but respectful distance, a male companion.

Down *there*, in the chaos of tangled wood,
blueberries thrust through inverted tree trunks,
wild flowers wait for the inadvertent bee,
things grow because they must,
                    as if by accident.
In this new orchard, and the measured garden
from which, an unapprenticed sorceress,
Hannah can fill her bounteous table,
there is a balanced order. The sun,
defying the thermodynamics of entropy,
provides the energy, the man and woman
the order, the choices, the impetus.

                        We turn,
and crossing the knee-high grass of the field
we are transfixed as a feathered shape
leaps down from a twisted shard of tree.
Amazed but curious, we circle it,
find a great owl with wings unfurled,
staring us down, holding a circle of ground
as a warning. No less surprised than we,
it turns its head in an impossible arc
to register the whole horizon of us.
We walk away. The curve of hill,
the sweep of grass, conceal us.

<118>

Later we sit, warmed by our red-bark tea,
and ask ourselves, "Was the owl hurt?
Was it protecting a nest? Why did it choose
to spread its wings and execute
that clumsy and alarming dance,
when it could have flown and vanished?"

I, too, dropped out of the sky to visit.
I do not know why I came.
My hosts are not just farmers
            but college folks,
the house has more books by far
            than pitchforks or rakes.
Ben talks about his research
            and the damn fools
who refuse to understand him;
I talk about my poetry
    and the damn-fool publishers who won't —
    you know the rest.
After dinner,
I spread *my* wings and dance
    the halting dance of my poems.
(Later I'll get a letter from him
suggesting I do something more practical
with the brain the gods gave me — ha!)

But for now,
night-bird and poet,
twine this rainy reunion
with our inexplicable presence,
knotting the thread of time
with an omen and a blessing.

<119>

THE CEMETERY BY THE LAKE

Edinboro Lake, PA

Day after day the sodden sky
refills the lake,
quenches the thirsty graveyard
with migrant tears
returning to the eye that wept them.

The used and tattered rain-clouds
come here like derelicts,
like old dogs homing, revisiting
one place — one secret lake
which has berthed all waters
(sea to sky to drawing
mountain peak in flash
of storm-drop) —

                 this unassuming
kettle of liquid clouds,
gray-black beneath
  the lidded heavens,
shimmers at night
  under the nodding Dipper,
  the stars that empty it
  of excess rainfall.

Now I come back to you,
wait for respite of thunder,
tread mud, walk flooded grass
to the neglected graveyard,
hark to the wind waves
at your overfilled edge,
the lapping song
of your careworn banks,
the hollow silence
of your glacier-ground heart.

<120>

Elms and maples stand sentry.
The ground is a riot
of toppled tombstones, limbs torn
by gale or lightning thrust,
fence pickets torn off
by age or vandals.
The winds — or cautious townsmen —
have removed the old gray trunk
that hoarded the shore like a sentinel
(how its unmoving spindle arms
alarmed the midnight visitor!
how ravens and owls perched there
to read the runes of the waveforms,
the prophecy of wind and season!
how poets and lovers sought it,
the artist's brush absorbed it
as silhouette defining the lake beyond!)

<121>

I miss that tree. If one of the graves
should vanish I would not miss it
so much as that withered guardian.

It was the life work of a living thing,
an epic of cambium in heartwood.
Its wisdom was sublimated from soil,
drunk from the lake of all waters,
tapped from the abundance of sunlight,
shielded from frost and lightning fire.

It made itself sculpture,
transcended its own passing,
a defiant singularity,
useless, unwanted, beautiful.

I shed my clothes to wade in the lake,
letting the chill-cold waters accept me,
sinking until the rippled plane of water
licks at my shoulders, pacing with caution
the rubble and sand of the lake-bed.
Not for a decade have I touched these waters,
communed with the throwaway songs
                of the bullfrogs,
the chirl of crickets, the paper-thin
presence of curious insects, the nudge of fishes
at my knees, the velvet black flurry
and sonar symphony of the bats.

Cars hiss by on the distant roadway.
House lights blink out. Water
goes lull, takes on the hues
of blueberries ripening —
black and gray and Prussian blue.

<122>

The loudest of sounds
is the breath in my lungs, my voice
as I call to you, lake of my youth:
Remember me.

I too have come back to this navel
of the world, this womb
of the waters, this quencher
of age and weariness.

Finally, your secret is revealed to me
in God's Eye weave of the thread of time:
the Eries came here for a winter festival,
carried a gourd with the old year's sadness,
weighted it with a stone, canoed
and dropped it at your quiet center,
singing —

Hear us, O Lake of Little Snows —
Heed not the crane, the fish,
the deceitful song of the serpent —
Heed us, mother of tears and rivers.
We bring you a gourd, the gourd
our ancestors taught us to make.
Surely you are hungry, O Lake.
We have come many days to offer it,
suffered such dangers to please you!

Calmly the lake accepted the present.
The gourd sank fast and never returned.
In silence, the men returned to the shore,
banked their canoes and shouted with glee:

Jiyathontek! O Konneahti!
Onenh, wete-wenna-keragh-danyon!
Hear us, O Lake of Little Snows!
Today we have made the signs.
Again you ate the gourd and the stone.

<123>

You did not know the gourd was hollow.
You did not ask what was in it!
Do not inquire, O Lake our mother.
We have promised never to tell you!

The gourd had passed a year in the longhouse.
Each mother who lost an infant held it
until the stream of her tears had dried.
The father who watched the forest trail
for the sight of the hunting party
clenched it and wept for his eldest son.
(They spoke of wolves at the council fire.)
In years of war or famine the gourd was heavy.
Women put beads or locks of hair inside it,
stained it with rust and blueberry paint.
Feeble ones took it when their memory failed;
it calmed the mad to sleep beside it.

Unburdened now of the Gourd of Sorrows
the Eries leave the forgiving lake,
wash off their paint, their red-brown
faces young with laughter and courage,
their eyes as bright as the ardent sun,
their strong legs running, running.

<124>

POEMS OF ANTIQUITY

ARIADNE

I've walked this edge
of solitude full circle now,
know it to be the island I am.
Sometimes peninsulas suggest
connection to land,
but sunrise never fails to find
me here, astride a rock,
the tide withdrawing
or coming in, the beach
a niche in a forgotten cabinet,
draped with the shorn clothes
of ocean, the false hair
of a reddened jellyfish,
the ribbon green of seaweed.

I launch my fragile bottles
into receding waves.
Inside, my letters beg
for a hasty rescue;
others are for the gods,
beseeching Poseidon

to dash and drown
the traitor Theseus —
the man who brought me
to this nowhere,

<125>

who lured me with promises
and sea-foam oaths,
who then abandoned me
for his sailors, for the first
prevailing wind to Greece.

My bottles dash
against the coral reef —
they break too soon,
or fall to the hands
of illiterate fishermen.

Here where this jagged mount
of Naxos scrapes sky,
harping a stone calliope
with fingers of wind, I wait,
far off the route of ships.
Someone below the horizon shall hear it.
Some ship will turn toward me.

Only a hero can avenge me.
Only a god can cancel
the vacancy of Theseus
that pulls inside of me
like an inverted birth.
In my dreams I begin to see him,
the purple sails of his galley,
his laughing eyes, the wreath
of grape leaves in his golden hair.

<126>

REMEMBERING MEDEA

This is Jason, not some ragged castaway.
By the wreck of the bold Argo, prow
shattered, Athene from mast absconded,
the bearded sailor sits on a rock.
The breakers tug at the rotting wood,
and though his blue eyes are deeper than sky,
his hair's a sooty snarl of salt and bile.

He is condemned to this harbor watch,
scorned by the citizens of Corinth,
comes from his peasant bed like a crustacean,
taking the scraps that the ocean leaves.
In the scant shade of his splintered ship,
more like a picked-clean skeleton of whale,
he whittles goddesses from galley oars,

<127>

mends his tunic with rags of sail.

The past is gone. The dangerous bride,
Medea, a motor of will, an engine
of blood and passion, dead. Their marriage
a ride on a horse that could never be tamed.

He always feared her,
though she never refused his mounting urge.
Yet loving her was thrusting manhood
into a cache of spiders, her womb
not silk but the clinging of arachnid webs,
holding him in until his terrified seed
exploded. She laughed, releasing him.
She shaved her pubic hair and burned it —
for power, she said. He saw the cask
of purple ointments beside her bed,
knew that the slaves of Corinthian wives
paid gold and precious stones for a daub
of them, knew how she used them
to turn his would-be sons and heirs
into those shriveled horrors she'd bury
in the garden at Hecate's hour.

Even the sons she gave him,
        she did so grudgingly,
tallying the hours of labor against him,
withholding her love and then inverting it,
slaying them to spite him,
snuffing them out like a casual abortion.

<128>

FRAGMENTS OF A HYMN TO RHEA, THE OAK TREE GODDESS

Earth-born Rhea   Queen of Oaks
Dryads' mistress and guardian
shelter and shade for the maidens three
who nursed the infancy of Zeus:

tender and virginal   dear Amaltheia
nubile and frantic   the dancing Io
withered and wild   dread Adrasteia

Oak in all your aspects   green-fired
in burst of spring   full-fruited
with pendant acorns   brown-limbed
and mourning on a hecatomb of leaves

A giant goddess   titanic oak
a sigil of your Titan origins

Still you echo   the thunder of shields
drumbeating spears   bare-shouldered Curetes
oak sons who guarded the infant god
baby in bird nest camouflage
stunned to silence by the tumult below

Your roots still plummet   to metals five
to mines of tin and lead and copper
veins of silver and fire-flaked gold

Mother of Gods and Sister of Titans
you it was who gave the stone to Cronus,
deceiving your cannibal husband
with granite wrapped in swaddling,
pretending to honor the infantophage,
blasphemer of the law of life.

<129>

It was you who raised the child in secret,
presented him as bastard cousin,
spawn of the lesser dwellers of ocean,
hostage cupbearer from trembling seas —
you who mixed the salt and mustard
into the nectar and watered wine,
you who stood by Zeus and whispered
words of courage and pride and waiting,
until the stupored Titan vomited,
disgorging the slimed Olympians
into the dark and cleansing river.

You were the lever that toppled your kind,
used wifely and cunning deceitfulness
to give the earth to the youngster gods.
And so you claimed a place in forest
took root and rest   welcomed the bird
the garland of clinging grapevine
zephyrs and rain   enduring the frost

sank roots when the moon was a baby,
saw it torn from the belly of ocean.
Then came the slant-browed hominids,
brutish but neither animals nor gods,
their first house built
in a lightning-scarred trunk,
first meal a windfall
of sweet brown acorns
nut-milk of your abundance.

Rhea, Rhea, Rhea!   Rhea, Rhea!
Hear the downward drumbeat
Rhea, Rhea   Pan cry
and lion roar   trilled chant
of your assembled priestesses.
Unveil us your mysteries
O red-haired Titaness,
acorn-jeweled Goddess!

<130>

Five-fingered leaves —
what are you saying?
Is this mad chattering
for mere birds only —
this frantic signaling
sign language of the Dactyls —
the virile thumb
the pointing index
the impudent finger
oracular, the tiny one —

Are you repeating the wind
or inventing it?
Are you teasing us up from apehood
with signs and mysteries?

You are silent as Saturn
with its leaf-dust rings.
Your scrolls fall everywhere,
a diaspora of scriptures.

I come to you alone   at midnight
I offer you   a Druid handshake
a subtle drumbeat   a melody.
Your great eyes open in rippled bark.
You do not speak.   You seem to sense
how men have toppled your ancient temples,
how forests are torn   birds dispossessed

You sleep again   but where your eyes
had studied me   the amber tears collect
the amber tears of Rhea

<131>

GANYMEDE

1

Night after night the pack of wolves came down
to stalk and ravage the peaceful flocks. Rams
fled and bellowed, ewes wailed while white lambs fell
and blood, black in the moonlight, stained the rocks.
Teeth gnashed at tender necks, bellies gave way
to serpent-sprawling innards, torn apart.
Dark silhouettes dragged limbs, ribs and gore
off to their own awaiting young ones. "Likos!"
                    the wolf-cry, made the blood run cold,
"Likos" made mothers reach for children,
elders to run for gorse-piles to increase
the fire that kept the hungry ones at bay.

At dawn, in cover of iron-gray clouds,
the men set out to find the lupine lairs,
hoping to slay the mothers and cubs,
then track and destroy the rest of the pack.
Never had so many wolves run wild;
never had so many flocks 'round Ilion
suffered such losses repeatedly,
as though a new kind of night-beast,
wily as man himself, strode on long legs,

feeding with jaws that never seemed
to fill a belly, as though they killed for sport,
Likos, then, or *likanthropos* —
                    the wolf that once were human?

The chief's son, young Ganymede,
too young to hunt, too gentle and kind
for the ways of killing,
remained at the shelter-cave with the women.

<132>

Tros took his nephews,
leaving his own son to guard the clan mothers,
the virgin sisters, the incoherent babes.
           One torch at cave-mouth would be enough,
           for no beast dared a burning brand.

All day, no enemies appeared.
Had not his mother thirsted for spring-fresh
water, had she not sent him with empty pouch
to the hillside source
(oh, as she later rued it!)
nothing might have happened.

But one low-hanging cloud which spread
from Ilion's walls to these high shepherd crags
was no mere storm — it was a god,
the dozing presence of Zeus himself,
who sometimes sleepwalks, unmoored from Olympus,
drifting from Hellas to the ends of Ocean,
or grazing the fire-tips of spouting Oeta,
or waking at the bruise of Caucasus,
scattering beneficent rain and the random strokes
of hubris-guided fire to some impious target.
Had not the thunder god awakened then
and seen the slender boy, filling the pouch
from the patient trickle of rock-pure water
(oh, how they wept and rued it!)
nothing might have happened.

<133>

2
The boy felt the tense of lightning poise.
His reddish hair stood on the nape of his neck,
his ivory skin, his eye-whites luminous.
He froze when the cloud unveiled itself —

A terrible eye regarded him
     from the black moil of suspended rain —
a place of cerulean blue, windless and calm,
the all-perceiving eye of the son of Cronus.

In one rock-rending thunderclap
     the heavens shattered.
The bowl of sky-clouds spiraled in,
the self-annihilating storm
consumed itself —

<134>

3

                    For that immaterial
blink-out the heir of Titans nearly ceased:
the strength to make a storm
was but the night sweat of his stupor,
the strength to *stop* one
a nearly impossible act of will
for even the hoary father of Olympus.

He caught his breath, feared
that the quake might tremble the arms
suspending the Earth from Chaos —

And then he hovered there, vast hawk
over hapless sparrow, assuming eagle spread
and talon grasp to assure the taking.
He pitied the tiny boy, frozen in his shadow.

No one had ever done this to Zeus —
no love at first sight for Io or Semele
(the prayers of suitors to Eros had scented
them out and lured a curious deity,
misunderstood by goddesses, to sample
the charms of mortal womanhood.)
But this was only a shepherd boy,
sprung from the loins of the chieftain Tros,
unsung in any lover's plea, a boy
whose beauty would bloom
for an instant as dew on hyacinth
or frost upon a frozen bowl —
a face, an eye, a cheek, a brow
so great as to transfix the storm
and make the mid-day Phaeton
    stumble in his headlong course.

<135>

Beauty too soft for marble, subtle for wood,
too unrepeatable to risk to memory,
too human to transform to star or shrubbery:
Ganymede, a happy accident of nature,
spared by the Fates until this imperious peak
of his brief, unnoticed existence.

<136>

4

It was worth the wrath of Hera
and the mockery of the wine-drunk gods.
"Zeus with a boy? A stripling boy!
Poor child, he'll waste away on arid Olympus,
turn to a withered ancient while Zeus
forgets him in one of his longer slumbers."

To their astonishment, the Titan forfeits sleep,
sends to the boy each dawn a cup
of nectar and a slice of Pomona's apples.

<137>

5

He summons the troupe of ageless gods
puts on his grey-beard visage and says:
"None but Ganymede shall bear this cup,
none but Ganymede shall serve me wine,
        and his the hands that pour clear water.
None but Ganymede shall turn the clouds
on which I rest and forge my thunder.
One tithe of my lot of immortal life I give
so that this boy will never age. His voice
will stay at the threshold of manhood,
his locks unshorn, his beard withheld.
He shall not shed even the salt of a tear,
immutable in my affections, semi-divine,
safe from the envy of goddesses.
Let him attend me always."

As seal of his oath, great Zeus displays
the form of Ganymede among the elder worlds,
joining the sun-path zodiac, the faithful boy,
star-striding Aquarius.

<138>

6

Ganymede feared the eagle.
He was relieved when great Zeus came to him
as the gray-beard god, almost a grandfather.
He came again in shepherd's robes,
younger by decades than before, hugged him
with great arms like a loving father.
Zeus laughed, then leaped into a waiting cloud,
his ever-ready tapestries and anterooms.
That night, he returned to the boy
    as a handsome youth,
fringed with first beard, tightened
    with muscle on arm and calf.

<139>

The boy did not resist, but let his hand
touch the hard lines of the lover's chest,
slipped to his knees in terror and awe,
not breathing when the athlete's body covered him,
thrilled with the priapic thrust against his loins,
not caring that a seed-burst could cinder him,
not fearing the rending of flesh by godhood.

And there was no pain — the ardent god
gave him, and took, a thousand pleasure strokes,
and every one was joy to both of them.
No one has ever been raped by a god.

<140>

7

Zeus steals again to look at the sleeping boy.
At last there is a question he cannot answer,
a riddle whose solving no manner of trickery
or Titan bluster could achieve. He asks himself:
Suppose I withhold a month of apples
from Ganymede? Suppose I let him age
just that much more? It maddens me
to hold a perfect Ganymede if Ganymede
plus Time were yet more perfect still.

The god turns sleepless on his mountain peak,
frozen between beauty and a mystery.

<141>

8
Ganymede thinks only of Zeus.
No one could imagine a greater joy.
And yet his delicate fingers shake
as he takes the green-peeled apple.
He puts it down on the golden tray,
looks at his blushing cheeks
                reflected there,
his hair still tousled by passion,
his lesser size, his frailer limbs.
He wonders: if I refuse the gift,
and let but one day's aging pass.
If I were older, fuller, stronger —
would Zeus love me better?

The boy turns sleepless in his sheltered bed,
frozen between love and uncertainty.

<142>

9

Hera paces outside the banquet hall.
Each night the men gods revel there:
Hephaestus, Apollo, blood-stained Ares,
Hades with his burning gaze, tide-worn Poseidon.
Each night they sing more merrily,
trade dangerous boasts about the Titan wars
as if Tartarus held no sleepers,
wax even stronger in their tales of love
for maids, and goddesses — and mortal boys.
Each night they leave, brawling with shields
and swords and tridents and staffs,
down to the waiting chariot hall,
until the room holds none but Zeus and Ganymede,
Ganymede and Zeus. For months, the goddesses
have been ignored and shunned.
Now Hera, the lawful mistress of marriages,
of love and hearth-fire parentage,
is banished to the kitchen of the gods,
the weaving room, the tending
of her temples. How long, she asks,
how long will this Olympian dalliance
preoccupy the lord of the gods?

<143>

10

I like to think of the gods still banqueting,
how they all came to love young Ganymede,
how Zeus neglected his Olympian rites
and ceased to trouble with the squabbling of gods.

I like to think of this summer storm
as the rolling of cloud from their lovers' bed,
as the never-tiring spark of their passion
rejuvenates this earth of forgotten temples.
I like to think of a joy that never dies,
of a beauty that never fades,

of a god's love transforming a boy,
of *all* manner of love enthroned
     and noble at last,
of love oaths written with stars.

<144>

11

I stand in the sorrowing wastes of Ilion.
By an eternal spring, I raise my cup,
in the shade of a lonely apple tree.
An eagle takes wing from a distant crag.
My heart cries: *Ganymede*!

<145>

THE RANSOM OF GANYMEDE

1

THE TEMPLE
They searched the mountains for the missing boy,
climbing the crags where the eagle might have
dropped him, scaling the ledgeless eyries
to which a bird of prey might home,
tearing through snow-filled crevices, risking
in caves the broken slumber of bears.
They came back mourning and empty-handed.
"I told you it was no eagle," the mother
intones. "A storm cloud *and* an eagle
seized him, the talons huge, the eyes
two holes of blue into the dome of sky."

The women attest to the truth of it,
how the terrible cloud came from the West,
how it cycloned into the giant bird,
soaring straight up with the rapted boy,
leaving an azure, cold and windless sky.
"You must go to the temple of Father Zeus
in Ilion," the women plead with Tros.
"For Ganymede's sake you must offer a gift.
Only the priest can secure his return."

Tros hated the town and its foreigners.
The row of marble temples alarmed him
        — the stone
and the statue of the Temple of Poseidon
blessing with trident and triton
the coming and the going of galleys;
the incense and dyes and jewelry
of Aphrodite and her painted whores
offering their charms to farmers for coins;
the older but unconvincing Temple of Zeus,
its edges wooden, its statue primitive —
a terra cotta king blackened by soot
from the greasy burning of entrails.

<146>

The chieftain puts on the anonymous robe
of a traveler, conceals his face in a hood
so that no rival tribesman might guess
his flocks were less than fully guarded.
He moves through the throng of the marketplace,
ignoring the vendors of drugs and statuettes,
the cripples and prophets and throwers of dice.

The priest of Zeus is aghast at the telling
of the charge against the son of Titans.
Yet no other god was quite so daring,
none other assumed the mantle of storm,
usurped the primacy of eagle with his own.

"It is the work of Zeus," he owns at last.

"What ransom can a shepherd offer *Him*?"

The priest shrugs. "A gift to the temple?
A tenth of your fleece for a handful of years?
An unspotted lamb from your choicest ewe?"
Tros spits upon the temple floor, his dark eyes
threatening. "What have those human bribes
to do with the lofty King of Olympus?
Would you trade my son for a bale of wool?
Since when does Zeus take hostages for priests?"

The priest withdraws his hasty suggestion.
"There is another way — deadly and dangerous.
A way to see into the mind of Zeus himself,
to know the fate of your beautiful son."
"I care not what danger. How is it done?"
The priest leans forward and hoarsely whispers,
"It is a way of madness and terror:
You must eat mushrooms with the Sibyl."

<147>

2
THE SIBYL AT DIDYMOS

It is a place of spiders, a floor
of sodden earth wriggling with lizards,
a moil of rodents, riddled with serpent holes,
a cavern shunned by the cleansing daylight
where the Sibyl's rising and sleeping obey
the urge and orbit of the moon and stars.
Her bed — a wooden casket gray and damp.
Her throne — a niche carved out of limestone.
Her food — a cauldron hung like a brazen bell
over the steam of a sulfur spring.

Tros stands his ground in the brimstone cave,
ignores the smell of mould, the nitre veins,
repeats his request to the shadowed crone,
"Sibyl, I come to eat of your mushrooms."
Her bony hands move to dismiss him,
the sleeves of her robe as stiff as stalactites.
Instead, he moves closer, until he can see
her prominent nose, her browless eyes,
the single hair on the end of her chin,
the tight lips framing her toothless jaws,
the knotted locks of her snow-white hair,
her Stygian complexion. "Do not persist.
Back to your hillsides, chieftain, go back
and do not meddle with the Olympians."

"Sibyl, I come to eat of your mushrooms.
I am your guest until my eyes perceive
the gods and what they have done to my son."

Her eyelids, stained blue to the semblance
of watchfulness, lift up to vacant sockets.
"Draw near, then, mortal, and be my eyes,
and I shall be your ears and speech.
We eat, and then we die and journey together."

<148>

3
THE VISION

Gold-headed Apollo greets them:
the red-haired chieftain and the eyeless crone.
He stops them at the very gates of Olympus.
Tros sees the blinding presence,
the cracked-voice Sibyl intoning the words
of the god appointed ambassador of Zeus.

"The King of Olympus asks me to say this
to honored Tros, future king, father
of the favored cup-bearer Ganymede:
A gift of two splendid horses I send you.

Know that your son still lives,
    immortal and loved among the gods."

<149>

"What would we shepherds want with horses?
And what can replace my only son? What
comfort can a mare and a colt and a mare's
colts be to me? My hearth-fire dies! No son
lives on to father my future. Lonely and cold
will I walk in the dim groves of Hades!"

"You are yet young," the messenger reminds him,
"and your line is fruitful. Take two more wives
from those who wait by the temple for husbands ,
and from them you shall father many sons."

"You know the future, then?"
                                        "A little,
just what the Fates let slip, trifles
for what they may avail you. For you,
with fire in your head and near-death
in your veins from holy mushrooms,
I'll open and read from the scroll of time...

"You have killed the preying wolf-pack — "

"Unlucky wolves, that cost me my Ganymede!"

"Take the skin of the she-wolf, Tros,
and keep it. It will hang on the wall
of your first stone house, in the hall
of your first imposing palace. Your men
shall take the skin and teeth and claws
of the lesser wolves, and make of them
their sign and war-dress. Wear them
in battle when you invade the town
of Ilion. You'll be its king in a decade,
no longer a chief of wandering shepherds.
Seek and drive out the human wolves
who clog its alleys and marketplace.
Restore the temples and their stolen treasures.

<150>

Punish the priests for their pilfering of gold.
Build an Ilion to stand through the centuries —
forget old times and call it *Troy*.

"Honor Poseidon. Welcome the stranger and his ships.
Join together the merchant and the Eastern caravan.
Beware of a beguiling princess from the West,
of strange machinery and Pelasgian tricks.
Build gates for Ilion — and never tear them down.

"I see more — even beyond the forgetting of Troy,
even beyond the blood-river death
of trickery and slaughter.

I see the she-wolf astride the central sea,
her sons the lords of all the known and unknown world.
But as the Egyptians say, this too shall pass."

"Enough!" cries Tros.
"Enough to know of sons and a city.
Who can conceive of an empire of cities?
No man should know what will be won or lost.
If they be better men than us who slay us,
        I too shall bow before the Fates.
I shall not seek out prophecy again.
If it seeks me, I shall slay the speaker."

Apollo laughs. "Tell no one, then, brave Tros,
but take these gifts, and with the wolf-sign
seize a city for your sons-to-be.

Great Zeus thus honors you and raises him,
your best-beloved Ganymede,
from mortal life to an immortal glory."

<151>

With this, the Sybil collapses unconscious.
Tros creeps away in silence, leaving a pouch,
his offering of coins and shiny stones.
Outside her temple he drinks from the spring,
          spits on the ground three times
          to clear the mushroom poison,
At last his head clears, his eyes resume
          their single-sightedness.
He is yet young, as the Sybil intoned,
          and he has great work to do.

<152>

HERA AND GANYMEDE

1

THE WRATH OF HERA

She's worn a path on the marble floor,
pacing the peristyle on summer nights,
storming about her Dorian palace,
dimming the lamp at the bedroom window
to watch the comings and goings
  at the gilded hall of Zeus.
Seldom does Hera receive his beckoning.
Her skin grows pale as Parian marble,
  her coif uncaressed
  as a spiderweb.
Her eyes grow dark as adders,
  her temper talon sharp —
nothing more terrible
than an unworshipped goddess!

For months the men have banqueted,
honoring Zeus and his Ganymede;
(months here, but decades below
where harvests blink on and off
like evanescent butterflies).
For months the boy has poured the wine,
    bare legged in tunic, unshorn
    his fleece of reddish curls,
    ageless and immortal,

<153>

enduring the seismic embrace
    of her husband,
the pinches and probes
    & cloudburst heavings
of the pleasure of gods.
Their drunken laughter stings her.
The boom of Ares shatters the din
    as he cries out,
"Again, Lord Zeus, kiss him again —
    see how the stripling blushes!"
Then laughter. Then silence.
Then the ominous strum of kithara,
    the piping flute of Phrygia
as the shepherd boy calms them,
singing a wild and plaintive melody.

The goddess chokes on the honey of sound,
the rising scale of the boy soprano
    neither man nor woman,
a thing of beauty frozen
in the space between genders.
She harbors her grudge for this
    (and many other slights)
like a stone in her innards.
She thinks of attacking him,
transforming the boy to a viper,
afflicting him with warts,
    painting his skin
    with venereal spots
    or leprous patches.
Or she'd lure him into a tryst
  with wily Apollo,
waken Zeus in time to catch them,
rouse his lightning to deadly ire,
folding her arms in satisfaction
as the boy was burned to a cinder.

<154>

Nor would this end the matter:
the wrath of Hera is no petty thing.
She'd send out bees to sting the suns
that sculpted the form of Aquarius,
erasing the boyish constellation,
rearranging the Zodiac
like a weeding gardener.
She'd send appalling dreams to Tros
of how the gods abused his son;
nightmares to Ganymede's mother,
the screaming fear of the sky-born eagle.
She could take no chances.
Forgiveness was unbecoming
    in a consort of gods.

Once, she had softened,
        turned Zeus' paramour Io
        back to maiden from calf,
        released her from gadfly
            wandering:
now Io was Isis,
        her alien temples
        undulating like snakes
        along the ocean shores,
and now the calm Osirans
        bleated their hymns
        of death and rebirth,
        an afterlife of mummies
            in incensed tombs.

She would not bear
    the dimming of her altar fires,
a change of her place in heaven,
the temple girls' gossip,
the wry mockery
    of faithless Aphrodite.

<155>

Yet Hera hesitates.
She knows the Greeks incline
to the easy love of boys,
war-making, the dirt of camp life,
to bluster and games,
true to nothing
but the tug of their genitals,
the primal urge pointing
them onwards and onwards.

How could she love them
if they were not what they were?

<156>

2
THE ENCOUNTER WITH GANYMEDE

It is a moonless night.
Earth dips into the inkwell sky:
even Olympus sinks
into the raven-feathered dark.
A chill blows up from the Stygian banks.
The smell of sulfur and stagnant ponds
usurps the garlands, the incense,
the overtopping urns of ambrosia.
The Greek Isles tremble.
Elephant waves stampede,
flooding the unprotected shore,
careening the ships in safe harbors.
The Titans roar in Tartarus,
bellow in their cursed sleep,
pulling their blankets of stone askew.
Zeus calls Poseidon. Ares arrives,
gallops from cloud-top
on his nightmare stallions,
armor akimbo. Lastly Hephaestus,
borne on a car with a clutch of weapons:
newly-forged swords and ancient javelins,
polished brass shields and helmets,
piled at the side of the council hall.

The earthquake wakens Hera.
She feels the crack on her temple floors,
the rush of mothers and children
to the shelter of her altars,
the supplication of priestesses.
Donning a cloak she rushes to the hall,
her hair and robes thrown wide
by the speed of her flight,
only to find the bronze door closed,
the brazier of welcome extinguished,
the servants scattering —

<157>

and there, trembling and pale,
the unprotected Ganymede.

She stops at arm-reach, throws back
the hood to show her visage —
the anima of Zeus, sister and wife,
head thrown back in arching pride,
matron and guardian,
all-seeing and unforgiving.

The boy looks up. A smile —
as if he knew her —
crosses his face and vanishes.
His green eyes pool with tears;
he sobs, leans back
against the hard unyielding door.

The goddess pauses astonished.
Surely he knows they are enemies?
Why doesn't he run, or scream for Zeus
to save him from her jealousy?
Is there some chink in the armor,
some serpentine doubt
   she could wedge between them?

"Do you know who I am, child?"

                                   "Well
            I know,
You are Mistress Hera, honored and feared."

"Then speak me the truth, favored boy of Zeus —
why now this weeping? I will not punish
your honesty."

            Fair Ganymede stammers,
his eyes averted in dread of her rage:

<158>

"I wept because I thought I saw — because
your face is the form of all mothers true —
because *my* mother has never seen me
since the whirlwind day of the eagle flight.
Her scream still haunts me. She must be old now.
She may not believe the Sybilene vow,
may think me dead or wasting, abandoned,

broken, the forgotten toy of the gods —
all while I take my ease on Olympus."

Again the Titans tumult in their beds
of lava, shed oily sweat, their coal waste spewed
into the terrified air. The firmament
trembles; a nameless star breaks free and falls.

Hera could kill him now, toss Ganymede
from cliff-high portico to rock below,
an accident, no witnesses (a bribe
would settle her case with the meddlesome
Furies.) But she pities him, shamed at her
spite for sake of the grieving mother.
Her anger turns from venom to milk.

She closes her eyes for worldly vision:
"Your mother is queen of a city now,
your brothers princes, your father's old tent
a torch-hung edifice of wood and stone.
They honor and revere you, Ganymede,
mourn for your manhood in the evening stars."
She regards him calmly, sees him at last
as another mother's son. "Still," she says,
"I would you had *not* come to Olympus."

<159>

3
GANYMEDE'S PLEA

Ganymede offers his apology:
"Ask all the Heavens, great Mistress Hera,
ask any god or spirit, ask zephyrs,
ask all who watch and listen down below
if ever in dream or prayer I wished
to be the friend and favorite of Zeus.
I did not summon him. I was no one.
He lifted me up to high Olympus.
He tells me he loves me; I believe him.

"He changes shape to please me endlessly —
bearded or smooth, boyish and soft one night,
perfumed ringlets of a singing Persian,
then hard as a Spartan he comes in armor.
He beams the white and gold of Apollo,
then Ares' copper cast and raven locks,
and then he towers black, an Ethiope.
He is a boy to my innocent boy,
then a man to teach me undreamt pleasures.
To think that Zeus has but one Ganymede,
but I, in one, have had a hundred loves!
I beg the clouds to part, the stones to sound,
the room to explode with his next surprise.

"And yet he still loves you, Mistress Hera.
Drinking, he swears an oath by you, calls you
Great Hera, the Old Lady, even his
good Old Lady. He always honors you
when hearing the vows of the jostling gods.
Knowing your name so loved, so highly praised,
how dearly I wish you did not hate me.

"I know that what I take from him is yours — "

<160>

4
THE RECONCILIATION OF HERA

Hera laughs,
becomes woman,
sits on the palace ledge,
places the boy at her feet,
not hiding the graying streaks
of her abundant hair,
the almost mortal wrinkles
framing her eyes.

"How foolish it is," she tells him,
"for gods to squabble for love.
There is love enough on Olympus.
If Zeus loves you, can you be less
than worthy? I thought you a whim —

<161>

a plaything, upstart and crude.
Jealous am I, but never so blind
as not to see the gold in the ore.
Eros may make a fool of men.
Down *there* a love-struck poet
    leaves Virtue abandoned
    for a day-blink Beauty,
wakes at the end of the dream
    with some screeching hag
    or a mop-haired stable boy.
Up here the light is truer:
    Beauty's a god
    the mere gods worship.
In you he must have found
that one pure moment of boyhood,
    some apex of youth.
So he has seized you.
Embracing you
    he spans the gap
    from what he was
    to what he has become.

"And as for sex,
there is ever more than enough
    of that to suit me.
You do not know why I love him.
My need for Zeus is a custom,
a kitchen thing, familiar,
an old cup to the fingers,
more onion than olive,
more fig than grape,
more milk than nectar.
His honor defines me.
He is husband and brother,
sharing the paternity of Cronus
and the oaken mother Rhea.
I am the cast of his embrace.

<162>

"He does not wish to plant his seed in me,
fearing the monsters I could bear him,
dreading the thought of a new usurper
I might conceal in some manger —

"Zeus knows that sex is nothing but trouble.
Once, when all the goddesses refused him,
    and all the cottages were locked
    on the sleeping earth below,
he pleasured himself on a cliff-side,
the show-off, erupting a lava flow,
so that Ocean bore him a likeness,

    spawned of his sperm and vanity —
    thus rose the rebel god
    fish-eyed and riotous,
    Dagon the terrible.

"Another time Zeus overcame himself,
thrusting in transport of a fevered dream,
and from his ear gave birth
to that know-it-all Athena,
owl of his eye and brainchild.
As for his mortal couplings,
    those night romps of lust
    that men gods shame me with —
imagine the brothel of crones we'd have,
    the moil of demigods,
if I didn't chase and undo them
each time he promises some village girl
    she'll bear another Heracles!

<163>

"It's really a mercy I turn them
to shrubs or birds or animals.
Sometimes the guilty scoundrel himself
transforms his mistress to thwart me,
adding another adulterous flower
to the botanica of Greece.
So keep his lust and proddings —
be glad you were not born a girl!

Keep his sweat and fondling of thighs,
the ache and release of his manhood —
only send him back to my hearth.
Let him nap on the bed he built me.
Let me be the mistress of Olympus
so that on earth the tender wife
remains the pole to her husband's lodestone.
So little do I ask of him."

Now it is Hera's turn to weep.
Her opal tears drift down from Olympus,
sink into earth and crystallize.
And so the Titans resume their slumber,
calmed by the chime of the singing drops,
locked in a silicon lullaby,
lulled to a coma by milky gemstones.

The bronze doors open. The gods peep out
to see the meek Aurora greeting them,
the sun car rising unthreatened by Chaos,
the shaken earth calmed, the men
already raising toppled pillars, the ships
upright and catching an early breeze.

<164>

They find the goddess Hera sleeping,
her head against a marble column,
beside her the nestled, dreaming boy,
head on her lap, his locks entwined
by the ivory fingers of motherhood.
Thus came an age of joy to Olympus.

<165>

THINGS SEEN IN GRAVEYARDS

FROM THE "THINGS SEEN IN GRAVEYARDS" CYCLE

1
THE TURK'S MAUSOLEUM

In monochrome Mt. Auburn
amid the pallor
   of marble and alabaster,
   ice pond and snow,
there is one burst of manic color:
a Turkish rug merchant's
      mausoleum,
   hung with a brilliant
   tapestry,
   sunlit from door-glass
   showroom bright.

His favorite Bokhara?
His last request
to keep it from Omar,
his rival, or Habib,
the brother he hated?

<166>

Or a ghoulish invite
to grave robbers?
Once in, the door slams shut,
and like a djinn, he rises.
Thieves have to hear
his well-oiled patter,
hours of rug talk,
gossip about the Iranians,
complaints about the
cheap carpets from China
that will be the death of him —

What business here
if you're not a buyer?

<167>

2
SACRIFICE

Before a cenotaph
in civilized Mt. Auburn,
we come upon
a desiccated squirrel,
his eyes a maggot nest,
his mouth
a frozen scream —

someone tore out his heart
and made him an offering
on the monument's steps,
legs extended
    into a blasphemous cross,
his vacant rib cage
crying "Murder!"

<168>

3
NIGHT WALKER
Still in her nightgown,
the wiry old woman,
nearly a skeleton in satin,
sleepwalked through lawns
onto a well-known path,
passing her mother's grave,
barefoot between the Civil War cannons,
out the back gate,
then down the slope to the river.

Imagine her walk,
untouched by thorn and burr,
oblivious to gravel,
then over rail and tie
without a splinter,
then gravel again,
then down the steep bank
to the summoning waters!

<169>

(Silt, fish, flotsam flow
from Youghigheny to Gulf —
how far might she go?)

Cats she'd once fed
watched from the dark
of rhododendrons
   but did not go to her.
I saw her, too,
   mute and astonished
as she passed the monument
where I had just recited *Ulalume* —

The cold chill current
did not awaken her,
lifted her up from her wading.
Weeds and crayfish
merged with her streaming hair.

She sank, her gown
a luminescent ribbon,
pulsing like a jellyfish,
for an instant ageless,
Ophelia or water nymph,
Rhine Maiden, Lorelei,
sparked like an electric eel,
and then the water
was black on black.
Her life dissolved
in unseen bubbles.

<170>

Who beckoned her?
What star deluded her?
What long-dead lover
   called from the mud
   of the river bottom?

<171>

4

NIGHT SHIFT
At two in the morning
three men pry the door off
of a well-kept mausoleum.
Their pickup truck,
concealed in moon-shadow
idles. I smell, from my hiding place,
    the acrid exhaust,
yew scent invaded by tailpipe vapors.
    They grunt
as a crowbar twists
the iron of a rusted lock.
One man advances
into the dead space,
stands with head bowed
as though in prayer,
    or hesitation.

The moon's full beams
illumine the chamber,
the urn, the wall plaques,
    a wreath
of shriveled camellias.
He waves the others in.
They shake their heads,
    don't want to do
whatever it is they are doing.

He puts his hands
    on their shoulders,
reminds them
of whatever it was
they promised.

<172>

He draws them in.
Together, they push aside
a stone sarcophagus lid.
They make a sickened groan,
spit epithets
in a language I do not
recognize.

They lift, drag something heavy
along the floor,
lift into pickup,
cover with tarp.

One man bends over,
heaves gobbets of puke
at the road's edge.
The other just laughs,
moves to the yew shrubs
to relieve himself.
He trembles, though,
    as he sprays the leaves.
Inches away, I hold my breath.
He staggers back, oblivious.

The truck pulls forward,
headlights doused.
The three men,
packed tight in the truck cab,
share a whisky bottle,
light one another's cigarettes,
wipe their hands on their
red plaid hunting jackets.

<173>

They watch for a long time,
wait for an interval
when no headlight is visible
anywhere, then race
for the gate and the streets beyond.

The door is left open,
  the crypt a shambles:
the open hole, wood fragments,
what might be someone's blood,
the broken lock.

I read the woman's name,
  Hungarian, I think,
  and her chronology —
  oh, a ripe one! —
    ten years dead,
ten years to the day.

<174>

5
TRYSTING PLACE

In August heat
  the fraternity boy
  slips out of his shorts,
  slides to the warmth
  of his eager girlfriend.
  They lay on a pioneer grave,
beach towel on a flat shale-stone,
  the lap of lake water
matching their rhythms.

Between the rising and falling
  as he stops
  to tease her wanting,
he reads the stones,
  lit up as headlines
  by the leering moon,
whispers inscriptions like names
of other women, better lovers:
  Jeanette...Sarah...Abigail.

The carpet of grass
seems to undulate.
The lake pulls back its waves,
the sky careens
above the maples.

He feels a host of faces
crowd inside him,
their compound anima
a cauldron of passions.

A diaphanous spinster
  clicks tongue
  against skull-teeth.

<175>

An ectoplasmic virgin
    blushes,
averts her empty
    eye sockets,
yet peeks through
double-skeleton finger fence.
A headless bosom
    envelops him.
Another's tree-root hunger,
roiling amid worms and centipedes,
rakes prickle-nails across his back,
    says *Love me!* —
                    Not her! — Me!

He stands — he screams —
his seed arcs out,
    a liquid aurora,
    dappling the grass
    in its fall.

"Someone — people —
    lots of them — watching!"
    he tells her.

Half-dressed, half trailing
jean shorts and underwear, they run
from the peeping ghosts,
the knowing grass,
the listening night.

<176>

6
MIDSUMMER NIGHT

I am well-met by moonlight:
Bats line the graveyard trees,
  hanging from pine and maple boughs.
  Not hundreds of bats,
      but *thousands* —

Their slant inverted eyes regard me.
 In their world I'm the strange one,
  a two-leg walker
      stuck to the ground,
dim-sighted, inarticulate,
deaf to their ultrasonic Sanskrit.

I love their wing-beats, their
startled flight when I clap my hands —
their comradeship for my monologues,
their brotherly listening —

And though they darken the trees
so the beacon moon,
the stars cannot intrude,
fireflies assemble
like landing lights,
my faerie pathway clearly marked
into the grove and the elder gravestones,
out to the lake and the quiet streets,
or — to nowhere

I can remain as their midsummer king,
a willing captive of Mab or Oberon,
regent of their passing luminance,
crowned in an aureole of foxfire

for this night of nights,
                    summer's briefest,
its joys packed frenzied, feverish,
from long-drawn dusk till
      teasing dawn
when batwings fold invisible
into the foliage and the ill-met
day people rise from their beds,
cock-crow, and assume their power.

Keep me now and forever,
    Thou sable Night!

<178>

7
WEST POINT

At West Point Cemetery
I come upon the grave,
the mass grave of cadets
who went half-trained
to a Mexican slaughter.
They lie in their shrouds,
      their dress blues,
      their buttons polished,
      shoes immaculate;
laid gently like babes
      in a playpen
side by side in a chaste
      embrace,
stacked up like logs
      for the burning,
smothered with loam and tears.
This ground is covered
      with yellow wood sorrel
the clover-like leaves for Luck
the frail blond flowers for Beauty
the persistent roots for Strength

I tear a stalk and taste
      its lemon flavor,
chewing it slowly —
not some pasty communion wafer
but a Host sublimed of flesh,
of hair and bone and marrow

not some dark wine fermented
by yeast in Original Sin,
but dew and rain and root-sap
drunk from the lips of the grave.

<179>

8
SALEM

At Salem
the burying ground
is a garden of stones,
an orchard of oaks.
Acorns burst to grow,
tombstones erase
their shallow tattoos,
becoming anonymous —

Death's heads
and angel wings,
bad poems
consumed by moss,
the promise of Heaven
like Confederate money.

Still there is *some*
justice — an oak trunk
engulfs the stone
of a solemn Puritan,
roots clinging like
rabid dogs.

He doomed the innocent
as witches and wizards,
to infamy and hanging,
to a farmyard burial
in family shame.

Imagine this —
his grave invaded
by inexorable roots,
the frail box split,
his gradual awakening
as vampire tendrils

<180>

invade his ears,
his mouth, his nostrils,
the circling of taproot
to snap his neck,
his arms and legs
broken and useless.

Doomed to immortal
consciousness
(the Life Eternal!),
nerves and ganglia
a web of pain receptors/

An old woman
condemned him to this.
She spoke the words
on a Candlemas midnight,
took from the hanging tree
where her mother's mother
died innocent,
the patient acorn of revenge.

She wrote his name on it,
pushed it with thumb
into the loam of his grave,
traced runes in blood
upon his stone,
danced the wild dance
of his resurrection —

sang things that the wizened
old ladies of Salem never knew
as there were no witches
in Salem
then.

<181>

9
THE FORGOTTEN GRAVESTONE

At Swan Point:
a level stone engulfed
by soil and grass.
It settled, perhaps,
or a careless groundsman
neglected it.

Most of the name is gone,
and half the date.
Earth closes like a wound
around it.

There must be no family,
no friends to make worried
inquiries at the office.

Perhaps he lived abroad,
fought an unpopular war,
was disinherited,
suffered excommunication,
the village homosexual,
married a foreigner,
died in a prison,
drooling lobotomized
in a madhouse,
morphined in an alley

or perhaps, he was a poet.

<182>

10
THE SWAN POINT GHOUL

Two months have passed
since I stood here,
in magic circle at the Old Gent's
grave, honoring Lovecraft.
The place I chose to stand on —
an older plot by a pine tree —
has dropped by a foot or more,
its earth a moil of root-turn,
brown against green
of surrounding sod.

Did the coffin collapse,
  or was it *removed*
    by something
    that tunnels
beneath the gravebeds? —
some necrophagic mole-man,
sharp claws on spatulate fingers,
red eyes sheathed in reptile layerings,
teeth jagged and piercing,
its sense of smell infallible,
burrowing from vault to tomb,
to late night lap of pond water,
to daylong sleep in a bat cave.

Even as we stood here,
      speaking our words of praise,
      reading our innocent poems,
did March earth muffle
      the splinter of casket
      the tear of cloth,
the insistent *feeding*
of the Swan Point ghoul?

<183>

THE McWILLIAMS' COFFEE TABLE

So the Joneses went out and did it:
took truck and winch and crowbar
and lifted a lamb-adorned
delicate gravestone
from country burial ground,

washed dirt and roots from its base,
set it on oak frame and casters
to be the life of parties,
the butt of jokes, the putting
down place of soda cans, iced tea
and sweating daiquiri glass.
Wine stains the pearly limestone.
Nicotine marks will not clean off.
The floorboards beneath
give off an ominous groan.

Torn between envy and outrage,
the neighbor couple lingers and gawks.
Mrs. McWilliams wants to report them
to the town and parish authorities.
Her husband Peter writes down the name,
Lilian McHenry who died in 18-
something, listens again as drunken Jones
retells the hazards of late night
shopping, guesses the town
where he made the heist.

"Hard work — and dangerous," McWilliams speculates.
"Like candy from babies," Jones boasts.

<184>

A new moon comes and passes.
It's party time at the McWilliamses.
And what should the startled visitors
find sporting a Chinese vase,
a *Vanity Fair* and a plate of brie?
An oblong box of Plexiglas
extending the length of the oversize sofa,
contains a sleeping beauty occupant —
none other than Lilian McHenry,
exhumed with care from her stoneless plot,
her long white corpse hair intact,
her long nails black, eye sockets
dark as six-foot soil
her shroud a study in tatters,
nose gone, gap teeth a hideous smile,
an onyx ring on her skeleton fingers.

Guests circle it cautiously,
noses alert for that certain smell,
eyeing the carpet for telltale stains,
dreading the thought of a sudden motion
within the griplock of polymer.

Soon enough the discomfort is over.
Lilian is adorned with coffee rings,
a spill of gin, a cocaine dusting.
The Jones parties are a thing of the past.
The McWilliamses so chic and clever,
so *au courant* in the finer art
of interior decoration.

<185>

SCENES FROM A MEXICAN VAMPIRE MOVIE

1

The vampire corners his nemesis.
Federico Van Helsing has lost the crucifix,
the holy water, the sacred Host.
His eyes gleam terror beneath his hat brim.

Dracula has an even bigger sombrero.
Each time he closes in, fangs extended,
their hats collide and rebuff him.
Castanets click on the sound track.

He won't take off the sombrero, of course:
a tiny bald spot on the back of his head,
a matter of pride and machismo.

"Next time, Van Helsing!" he swears,
retreating. "Next time I'll get you!"

<186>

2

He flees the bedroom of Doña Lucia
in haste when the rooster crows.
The lady was willing, the duenna
hypnotized. But they spent all night
shifting the statue of the Virgin,
turning the holy paintings to the wall,
unnailing the crucifix over the bed,
removing the Bibles. He counted
a dozen rosaries between them,
paced and smoked a long cigar
as they untangled the jangling beads,
trying to get the lady undressed
and ready. Hungry and pained
by the lambent sunlight he curses
them, bursts into a cloud of mist,
drifts out the open window.

"Wait, oh wait!" cries Doña Lucia,
"I'm almost ready!" Just two more
rosaries to disentangle, just one
more necklace with the Sacred Heart —
these modern vampires just don't
appreciate foreplay!

<187>

3

Things go wrong
at the American border.
The vampire's coffin is opened,
the soil sifted by guards
snooping for cocaine,
for seeds and sprouts of pot.
They rip the casket lining,
for suspected bags of heroin.
They shrug, wipe dirt
from his Transylvanian grave
on their trousers, wave
the hearse through. The coffin
is a shambles. His priceless
soil drifts out, the deadly

rays of sun intrude.
His castle reduced to
a leaky shanty,
entering California like an Okie.

<188>

4

Lucky for him, he flew north,
his bat wings skimming the Rio Grande.
He plans to meet up with his coffin later.
A furtive wetback supplies his dinner,
a slash and suck, fast food *al dente*.
He meets the hearse at the rendezvous,
listens smiling to the chatter of the driver,
the bug-eater Renfeldez, who drools
describing the L.A. cockroaches.

He takes a hammer to repair his coffin,
smooths the layer of native soil,
crawls inside with the worms and spiders,
inhales the rich aroma of humus,
the faraway sunset of Carpathia.

Above them, the Immigration helicopter
follows the hearse northward.
"Just that weirdo with the coffin,"
the pilot argues, "We checked him —
he's clean."
            "Not him," the other
replies. "The guy in the black poncho,
the big sombrero, the guy he picked up
in the middle of the desert.
We got it all on the infrared.
Let's go down and nab 'em!"

Renfeldez puts down his tequila,
hears the descending chopper,
awakens the master.
The wide-winged bat flies up
to meet them. Nowhere to run,
no crosses or garlic at a thousand feet,
the pilot and officer are easy prey.

<189>

Never knew what hit them or how
a bat could change to a wolf,
tearing them to pieces,
lapping hot geysers of blood,
letting the aircraft fly drone
toward the pink horizon.

He settles back into casket
a smile on his blood-caked lips.
He likes these Americans,
the taste of cattle in their veins,
the malt of beer, the well-fed
plumpness of their bodies.

He sleeps to the croon of Renfeldez,
warm in his poncho,
eager for the hot nights of L.A.,
the cool fogs of San Francisco.
Over the lid of the coffin,
concealing the Dracula crest,
his blood-stained black sombrero.

<190>

HE'S GOING TO KILL ME TONIGHT

1

He cannot sleep. His feet
are cannonballs on creaking boards,
the wind's maniacal, the trees
a troop of palsied tap-
   dancers on glass.
His eyes lockbolted awake
   his ears, electrified,
   are microphones
   set close to feedback screech.
In amber light of dusty lamp
   he reads the note
   that someone crammed
   under his door
in spidery script:
He's going to kill me tonight.

Midnight. The Reaper's shift begins.
The minute hand tips past Reason,
careens into Murder's tithe of night.
Somewhere a gloved hand
   drops bullets into grooves,
   revolves an oiled cylinder,
   tenses at trigger touch
Somewhere a knife attains
   its hairsplit edge,
   rasping against stone,
   then like a snake
   into its coil'd hole,
   slithers into scabbard
From somewhere he hears these sounds
   (or doesn't hear them)

<191>

Who wrote the note? The blonde
on the floor below? Perhaps a pimp
she worked for has threatened her?
Perhaps a rescue and runaway in store?
He pictures the two of them in strange hotels
glued together on a blanket with spent passion.

But no, she moved a week ago. He groans
at the thought of the penthouse transvestite.
He calls her Desdemona she's pasty white —
the Haitian night watchman beats her on Saturdays,
a noisy ritual for a weekend Othello.
Who else could it be?

The children's librarian in 19-A? (She tried
to get him to fix her stereo last week...)

He cannot guess who it is. The roaring truck
and raucous sanitation crew earthquake
and cymbal crash the building front, so loud
they would muffle a silenced gun, a choking,
the moan and gurgle of heartstab mortality,
the fall of a chair beneath a noose.

He wonders if it happened just now.
He would never know until the newscast,
unless the squad cars clogged the pavement.
Which one? Which door would open on death?

<192>

2
Across the hall, the spinster lay in her bed,
breasts taut against the tightened sheets, hands
folded expectantly on throbbing heart.
She will be eighty-five next week.
Her knotted fingers wrote the warning note.

The window is open, the burglar gate unlatched,
the door unlocked and welcoming.
She waits for the man who is coming to kill her:
the grocer's boy, the laundry man, the super,
the mailman from Ponce, the plumber from Manila.
She waits for the man who is coming to save her:
the neighbor who smiles and helps her with packages.

The garbage truck covers his footsteps.
She grips starched sheets with painted nails.
The faces of killers and saviors begin to blur.
A streetwise silence sweeps after the garbage men,
sleek as the fur of an alleycat, stilling the air
save for the random scuttle of paper scraps, the roll
of soda cans, the rasp of a leaf against gutter,
the indefinable tread of the storm drain rats.
The wind invades the curtains, jostles her hair.
Her tears well up at the silence of fire escape.
No one has ever touched her.
No one ever will.

<193>

THUNDERPUSS: IN MEMORIAM

VIGIL

A Lucretian Ode
for Thunderpuss the Cat

The cat is growing old now; her
fifteen-year-dry fur comes out in tufts
when I brush against her. She sleeps,
limps to the litter box, takes naps,
samples the offerings in the food dish,
enjoys a siesta, laps from the cool
clear surface of the water bowl,
goes back to the stovetop,
the heater, the waiting electric blanket.
Her eyes roll back,
    she twitches in dream pursuits.

She is queen of a Siamese jungle.
Ferocious toms preen and wait their turn
to woo and mount and pleasure her.
Birds fall from the palmate trees,
their rainbow plumage in her jaws,
the taste of blood from a heart
      still pumping,

beating the terror and agony of
   being devoured
     by Beauty.

I come upon her limp, unmoving state,
sprawled on a towel on radiator top,
her head suspended in air.
Carefully I check for her breathing.

<194>

Any day now, she will cross over
    into the crystal dream of unbeing,
stalking the perimeter of organic life,
sublimating from neuron to ghosthood.

It is a fitting vigil. She taught me this.
On those rare days when I would pause,
to sit inert and motionless,
she'd pad toward me in bristling alarm,
leap on my lap, creep up my chest,
place her cold nose to my nostrils
to check for *my* breathing,
tapping my cheek with her padded paw
as if she knew that life is motion,
that there is not a moment for idleness
between the two abysses that punctuate
the brief pincushion of consciousness,
that even sleep is an exercise,
a boundless leap, a chase,
a love affair where everyone
says "Yes" and does it again,

that imagination is motion, too —

It is said that animals know little of death,
yet this venerable cat must sense it,
the creeping twilight in her veins and limbs.
She will not cease moving with joy,
she will try to continue,
the poem of her purring
a motor perpetual, her Siamese talk
longer than the tale of the Nibelungen.

<195>

We keep our vigil against the time
of no moving, fearful of stopping,
dreading the hooded figure,
yet knowing that if he exists
he is ahead of us, waiting,
that the more we flee from the past
the sooner we meet the ordained
or accidental terminus —
But this, you say, is a house cat,
not the loved and lost Lenore —
Animals are put to sleep,
animals are killed and eaten,
animals consume animals —
why should the imminent end
of a pet produce these
mortal intimations?

Because every death partakes of Death
and teaches us to surmount our human terror.
It is not the end that matters.
An eternity of unbeing preceded me,
an eternity of nothingness will follow.

The only appropriate answer to the universe,
to the void that makes and swallows us,
is to leap and strive and dream,
sing to the cosmos with animal joy:
"I live. I move. I know. *Thank you.*"

<196>

THUNDERPUSS: IN MEMORIAM

(1971-1987)

1
At the end
you are lilac —

sun filters
through holes
in the carrying case —

frail lilac
tinged on white

your fur
a rumpled coat
no longer sleek
on skeleton

legs too weak
for running now,
your leaps
misguided
end in confusion
yet you are lilac still
eyes blue
as Siamese skies.

You come out of the box
all kitten,
ready to explore,
eager to know,

<197>

yet terrified,
into the hands
of the doctor

2
Print shop cat
tracked through open ink cans
to autograph
the works of poets
with indelible paw prints.

Always underfoot
intractably neurotic
from the start

an all-night howler
in heat more than out

toms on the roof
        at the cat-door window
toms taking turns
working in shifts
not even bothering
to fight
for your inexhaustible
yearning

steel spring queen
of a city of orgies.

<198>

3
Your leaps
were prodigious —

from floor to door-top

straight up curtains
bookshelves like ladders

<199>

nothing would daunt
your interest in ceilings,
high places,
hunter's eye view.

Even the ledge
between two office windows
too narrow for turning
did not defeat you —

you simply walked backwards,
regained the sill,
jumped to the floor
like a film in reverse.

4
From hellcat
you grew civilized,

calmed to the sound
of Handel and Mozart,
sat rapt at the foot
of my harpsichord,

tempered the leaps,
the claws-out landings.

A gentle reminder
from a water pistol
cured you of scratching
the furniture.

You grew to dignity
yet never shed the pride
of an aristocrat.

<200>

No one could pick you up
yet you would deign
to throne a lap
with your presence,

accept a suitable interval
of petting,
the obsequies
that mortals owe
to incarnate beauty.

5
Dreaming
      you were more real
than waking

dreaming
      you could escape
      the dull perimeter
      of print shop
      of studio apartment
      of four rooms in New Jersey

to pad a crystal jungle
      stalk forest floors
      cross deserts
      converse with demons
bask in a sun that never sets

await the arrival
of your leopard king
whose sleek black fur
and amber eyes

are your eidolon
of Beauty.

<201>

I watched you dreaming:
the twitch of eye,
the paw extended,
the clench and unclench
of your jaws
tried to imagine the place
that lured you,
its feline geometry
one leap beyond
my human faculty.

I'd wake sometimes
to find you sitting there
upon my chest
eyes huge as moons
staring   staring —

perhaps you too
brooded
on sleep and death,
waited for my
awakening
and asked yourself

Where does he go?

<202>

6

Only a grudging carnivore,
you were happy
with that bloodless stew,

those maddeningly crunchy
stars and tidbits,

those tins of neatly
chopped and compressed tuna.

Once, growling with
animal rage, you came back
with a mouse in your jaws;

once, the house was filled
with sparrow feathers;
now and then, you'd catch
and swallow something
with too many legs,

run for the water bowl
to wash it down.

But near the end
you sat on sun-porch
surrounded by finches
and feeding sparrows

no glint of killing
in your blue eyes
calm as a storybook saint
preaching to wildlife

pensive as a Buddha
counting the sunfalls
toward Nirvana

<203>

7
We became one person,
shards of the same crystal,

mirrors
of one another's moods

you were always there
   protesting my absence
   before the key
      could readmit me

you at the end
   of every journey

running to rustle
   of grocery bag

someone to shop for
      catnip at Christmas
      a rabbit-fur mouse
      a length of twine
      a boneless breast
         of special chicken

<204>

8
A burglar came
through the downstairs window.
I frightened him off —

black leopard man
with amber eyes
leaped from the porch
over the fence
gone like a nightmare.

I wanted Death
to stalk you silently,
visit your sleep
like that intruder

surprise you gently,
take you from me
like a thief.

But when I find
that you can barely walk,
that you will not eat,
see you convulsed with seizure,
I must become
the agent of Death,
must temper him
with kindness.
I did not want
to choose the time
of your going.
Making the appointment
I gasped to spell
my name to the clinic,
shaking with grief
and more than grief.

<205>

It was not done in a daze.
The sun was brilliant.
Cats watched from every window
as I walked with blue box
toward the clinic.

It was the third of September.
Summer had died in the trees
the night before, blinked out
like Merope, the lost Pleiad.
Stars burned invisible
over the daytime sky.

I talked nonsense
to your moaning
    jabbered about
    going for a walk
    calm down
    we're
    almost
    there

<206>

9
Your absence
is palpable

like nerves
to an amputated limb
I still feel you
about to step
around the corner
of the sofa

hear you leap
from stovetop
to chair
to floor

the silken rustle
on carpet
claw clatter
on floorboards.

But these presentiments
are false now:

you are dust mote
rising to icy air,
a final leap
into unbeing,

you are ashes,
gray with a hint of lilac.

<207>

AT LOVECRAFT'S GRAVE

AT LOVECRAFT'S GRAVE

On the Fiftieth Anniversary of Lovecraft's Death — March 15, 1987

1
That does not sleep
which can eternal lie,
yet Howard, Old Gent, *Ech-Pi-El,*
Lovecraft who signed himself
Grandpa and Theobaldus
to his fans and correspondents
most assuredly sleeps here.
We drift into the vale of earth,
the gentle falls and slopes
of Swan Point Cemetery,
gather to remember and praise him
as the Seekonk with its silted memories
ribbons at the edge of vision.
The sculpted monuments
    of angels and Psyches
repeat the largesse
    of immortal promises —
not so for his simple stone

placed forty years too late
to help his absent-minded shade
come home.
            Yews and cedars
bluff Ides of March
with bitter green, droop branches
like soiled wigs, while honest

<208>

bare branches of a spreading beech
retell the long years' chase of sun,
the repeated losses of winter.
Which is the emblem of Lovecraft's sleep?
His life lays stripped
    as that sorrowed beech
    where his initials are carved
    (real or spurious?)

his nightmares the evergreens,
    lingering through seasons,
    harboring night-wing
    as readily as lark.

<209>

2

We stand about, a handful
swelling to nearly a hundred,
trying to envision his folded hands,
his hand-me-down Victorian suit,
wonder how much of his habiliments
have fed the indiscriminate hunger
    of the conquering worm,
his eye sockets empty and dry
    gone beyond dreaming
though we close *ours* and see
the tower of ageless Kadath,
the shark-infested ruins of Ponape,
the imaginal Providence
where he walked arm-in-arm
with Poe and his eccentric Helen.

Our Lovecraft, lord
of the midnight shudder,
eaten from within
by the gnawing shuggoth of poverty,
the Azathoth of squamous cancer,

the loneliness of Nyarlathotep,
drugged by nurses into the sleep
where dreaded night gaunts fly
and bent flutes warble
a twisted melody —

and yet he faced it stoically
  like a proud Roman,
  an 18th century gentleman.
Death came with burning eye
  and found him not trembling,
never recanting his cosmic vision,
waving away the white-collared cleric
    with a wan smile.

<210>

3

Hundreds of miles we came today
to pause and pay homage,
readers and scholars who have leafed
his books, studied his papers,
debated his sources and meanings,
tread in his footsteps in Gotham
and Boston and Federal Hill,
stood with a thrill
      at his one-time door.

In sorry, mean-spirited Providence
no plaque or marker reminds us of him. [1]
His grandfather's estate an apartment house,
his mother's house vanished,
his last abode uprooted and moved
like an aimless chessman on street map,
as though the upright town
      with its sky-piercing steeples,
      mind-numbing priests,
would like to erase him.
 A baby in mother's arms
intrudes on our reminiscing,
breaks Carl Johnson's eulogy
with gurgles and cries of
R'lyeh! Wah! R'lyeh!
(shunned name of the city of doom
where multi-tentacled Cthulhu
dictates his madhouse symphonies!)

As Joshi reads sonnet
      the sun blinks off
behind a humped shoulder
      of cloud,
and the air turns cold,
    unnaturally cold
in a spell of seconds.

<211>

Earth reels beneath our feet
into the chasm of sunless
        space.

4
Ah! this *is* the moon's business,
or the work of a moonless night.
Should we not speak of him
        beneath the glimmer of Hyades,
the velvet pall of the void,
the primal ether in which the cosmos
whirls like a raft into maelstrom,
the vast interior spaces
        of Time and the Angles
where the gods as he knew them
        drool and chant?

But they will not permit us
        to assemble by night.
They seal the gates
        against our ghoulish
        intrusions,
pretend that the coffined dead
        cannot be heard
to turn in their neglected
        crypts, deny
that lingering essences

        drawn from the memories
of the living can take
        an evanescent life —

pale shadows of shadows,
        reflected gleams
from the dusty pane
        of a mausoleum,
glints from polished granite

<212>

or marble,
a sliver of sourceless light
in the eye of an owl
    or a raven;

pretend we are not
    untuned yet powerful
    receivers of thought,
    transformers of vision,

as if we did not know
how night
    vibrates with poetry,
    eidolons plucked
from the minds of the dead.

Reporters and camera crews
take us in warily,
eye us for vampire teeth,

    chainsaws, machetes,
    jewelry and witches' teats,
wonder what crimes we lust
    beneath disguises
to perpetrate
    upon their babies,
    their wives,
    their altars.

We smile,
    keeping our secret of secrets,
how we are the gentle ones,
how terror
is our tightrope over life,
how we alone
    can comprehend
the smile behind the skull.

<213>

5
Later a golden moon lifts up,
swollen with age and memories,
passing the veined tree skyline,
leaving its double in Seekonk,
disc face scanning the city —
the ant-farm of students on Thayer,
the tumult of traffic on Main,
the aimless stroll of dreamers,
dim lamps of insomniacs,
the empty, quiet graveyard
winking like a fellow conspirator
at the prince of night.

Dimly on obelisk
a third moon rises.
The offered flowers
against the headstone
quiver and part.

A teenaged boy,
backpack heavy
with horror books,
leaps over the wall,
eludes the sleepy
    patrol car,
comes to the grave,

hands shaking
frightened,
exultant,
hitch-hiked all day,

<214>

waiting,
mouthing the words
of *Necronomicon*,
for a sign
that does not come

the clear night,
the giant moon
throbbing
as he chants:

That is not dead
which can eternal lie,
And with strange eons
even Death may die.

<215>

LOW TIDE

"The tide was flowing out *horribly* — exposing parts of the riverbed never before exposed to human sight . . . *something* descended to earth in a cloud of smoke, striking the Providence shore near Red Bridge . . . The watchers on the banks screamed in horror — '*It* has come — *It* has come at last!' and fled away into the deserted streets."
— H.P. Lovecraft, letter dated May 21, 1920

"brisk off-shore winds pushed a lower than normal 'moon tide' even lower on Narragansett Bay . . . miring dozens of pleasure boats in a sea of mud . . . There are mechanics who say that in the 20 years they've been working here, they've never seen anything like it." — *Providence Journal*, September 18, 1986

The azure sea, the silt brown Seekonk,
the placid ebbing of sun-tides,
the contrary pull of the moon,
all form a subtle balancing act —
until accumulated rhythms
resolve in one great tug
at the sleeve of the world.
The sea withdraws, the shape
of the earth convulsed by gravity

as if the sentient waters
grown weary of poison and oil slicks,
bereft of the colloquy of whales,
shrugged into space.

Would not the war-hemmed
Mediterranean be more serene
refreshing the cracked canals of Mars?
Would not the North Atlantic,
brimful of nuclear submarines,
prefer to slip off the earth-edge weightless,
an unmissed flotilla of icebergs
writing their names in the velvet sky
as comet messengers of Chaos?

<216>

The Narragansett waters drop
as the ocean makes its getaway,
rivers run dry
to fill the falling shoreline.

Drawn from their sleep by the burning moon,
the people, a motley of coats and robes
and slippers, a clot of bicycles and skates,
drift down to the riverbank
to see the helplessly stranded boats
dangle from their moorings,
level with their anchors,
topsy-turvy on a forest of pilings,
sails drooping and torn,
their rotors exposed like genitals,
their captains perplexed and swearing.

The riverbed undulates with dying fish,
the wriggling of eels in the hardening mud,
the half-seen slurry of amphibians.
Around the base of the iron-red bridge,
the barrows of humanity emerge:
a tangle of cars and mattress springs,
the skeletons of suppressed babies,
a statue of the Holy Infant of Prague,
a well-preserved gangster in a steel drum,
a thousand soda bottles & aluminum cans,
and, standing up like autumn trees —
or some hideous joke of the fishes —
the unfurled frames of lost umbrellas.

Someone says the water will return,
Low tide out, high tide in, insists
the river and the bay and the sea
will repave themselves with reflected sky.

<217>

Then why should a fireball plummet down
into the sodden riverbed? They watch,
hoarding their fears in the windless midnight,
as steam subsides over the mud-lined crater.

A madman, barefoot, bearded, rag-robed
avers that the Kraaken is rising
from the noisome mud on the bottom —
He snatches a fisherman's lantern
and runs across the Red Bridge screaming
"*It* has come! *It* has come at last!"

The people hear a distant murmur. A child
goes rigid with the spasm of seizure.
A woman faints, and no one leans
to pick her up. It is a blur
of stumbling and clawing: a boy
is struck down cold for his bicycle,
a deaf girl trampled near a street light.
Men break the door of the great-domed church,
determined to pray out the end of the world,
encircled by Host and holy books.

Of course, it is only the tide returning,
the meteor a slap from the brittle stars.
Homesick and dizzy from errant flight,
the prodigal sea comes home.
The boats resume their proper angles.
The bay fills in, the river rises.
The elders of Angell Street will say
None of this ever happened.

<218>

MIDNIGHT ON BENEFIT STREET, 1935

Three hundred years ago it was a footpath
winding among family grave plots —
moved, all moved —
    at least the *stones* were moved —
to pave and straighten.
Now it is a strange amalgam
    of mansions and squalor,
every other streetlight shattered,
every other doorway an entrance
    into vice and delirium.

John Brown's mansion lords over the street,
aloof at the end of its ponderous lawn,
high fence upon a looming wall
so you are always beneath them,
going about your business unnoticed.

Ear pressed to those stones,
what might you hear
beneath the slurry of earthworms —
what muffled groans and chain-clanks?

Or maybe the slip-slide of silk
upon the polished floor, the fumbling
for a long-forgotten key
to the snug merchant cabinets and cubbyholes
stuffed with lost bags of silver coins?

<219>

In the stillness of museum night,
the mummy shifts in its linens,
dry lips stirring in natrous dust.
The stolen Buddha's hand creaks slightly
as it regards its empty palm
with a wooden eye turned suddenly
as bright as the orb of a tiger.

Fireplaces puff out the acrid smoke
of exterminated forests, ash falls
in minute flakes, snow's prelude.
The brooding Athenaeum
thrusts up its temple front,
a vault where books
    and the ideas within them,
slumber untouched for decades.

<220>

tended by
    frowning priestesses.

A hurried shadow passes
    the darkened Armory,
a faint air of rust
    and dampened sulphur.
Long past the freighting time,
    the railway tunnel
    beneath the street echoes
    the shout of a drunkard,
    then silence — no,
    not silence —
    the chittering of rats,
thousands down there
in daily migration
between two rivers.

Does he linger now
before that house
whose double cellar doors
fronting the sidewalk,
where phosphorescent fungi
alarmed his boyhood visits,
and feral scurryings
bred nightmares
of things that gnawed
behind the wallpaper?

He keeps the Capitol in sight,
and overhead, a crescent moon,
and there! a scintilant Venus,
forming a triad with Regulus,
up in the lair of the Lion,
this night of all nights of the year.

<221>

And there, the steeple
    on distant Federal Hill,
St. John's, the Starry Wisdom place.
If only the worshippers knew
what secrets slept above them!

He passes, too, the house in red,
the garden of roses where Poe
first saw the Helen of Helens,
the dark-paned parlor of wooing,
the door that finally
    barred and denied him.

 He looks down to the ruined waterfront,
past the Episcopal churchyard
to the silted river, the rotting wharves,
the sullen, silent warehouses
that once burst with silks and tea.
In one of those dim taverns Poe
recited "The Raven" for a whiskey.

Somewhere down there
in a Chinese alley
lay the way to Eldorado
or the Valley of Dreams —

but no, these are modern times —
there is nothing down there
but a wallet-snatch beating
for a solitary poet.

Howard Phillips Lovecraft
turns back homeward.

<222>

OCTOBER THOUGHTS IN WAR-TIME

What does October mean?
 To the old Bolshevik the month we finally took what was
    ours —
 to the old émigré the month we lost everything,
 and had to flee to the border.
To the Spanish and Portuguese, Italians and Greeks,
taking café in treeless plazas,
the aftermath of equinox, a few brown slurries of oak leaves
skittering from Alps to the sea, not a time, but a passing,

To the Chinese, a mottled dream of maple, gingko,
ailanthus and willow, in which one pale
and angular scholar, his beard as thin as an artist's brush,
takes tea in his gazebo, as the autumn's white tiger
runs down the bounding deer.

For me, in this New England city,
it is not quite autumn.
I spy the moon's new crisped crescent
hovering above the Hopkins house.
An angry Mars is at its nearest —
all these heavenly bodies tugging at treetops.

The Unitarian bell tolls eight, as Uranus,
a dim flickering, grazes the steeple
as though curious to know
for whom the clabber sounds the bronze.

The weary earth has had enough explosions.
Winter will yield up autumn,
if autumn will erase its merry carnage.
If leaves do not fall, perhaps the heads of state
will leave decisions undecided,

<223>

prisoners   un-decapitated,
toxins   unmanufactured,
uranium   un-enriched —
perhaps the deadly elements
will go unmined, the gray bombers
unmanufactured,

the hateful thought, snug in its walnut,
from its high branch
unfalling.

<224>

LUCY: A MYSTERY

Vacant heart and hand and eye,
Easy live and quiet die.
—Sir Walter Scott

I.
The bar in Poe's hotel, a proper bar
with deep mahogany paneling, row
upon row of wines to savor, great casks
of low-grade by-the-barrel rum, ales
unheard of except this close to the sea
that brought them — thumb-nosed and snug
        in the sight
of the disapproving First Baptist Church.
Let Roger Williams frown, the ladies
of the Temperance Society petition:
in vain since the long polished bar was lined
and elbow'd by half of the town's lawyers.
Rank upon rank of tables, niches and corners
sufficed for the lower sorts: workmen
in coveralls to the lean, carousing sailors
ear-ring'd in gold and of uncertain parentage.
Poe sat with Pabodie, a celebrated local,
a delicate man who had read at law
but had no taste for the practice, a poet
with a melancholy ode or two within him,
but above all a useful man, a man who knew
the nature of men and everyone's business,

a man to sound out about the Power family
whose elder daughter, a widow named Helen,
a poetess, he had come to woo.
An answer discreet affirmed her fortune
a small one, but reliable: property and mortgages,
well-managed by old Baptist lawyers.
Eyes rolled slightly around the bar
as Poe asked about the late Mr. Whitman:

<225>

a literary man, to be sure, a lawyer
who defended atheists and defamers
of preachers, a man of calamities
whose winter cold went pleural, and killed him.

And as for Sarah's father, "Ah, the less said,"
was all that Pabodie would offer. "And there's
a sister we don't speak much about." Poe felt
unable to pry more from Pabodie, at least
so long as he remained this sober. Gossip
is best pried with the lubricant of wine.
Poe talked instead of his earlier visit,
the summer of '45, of the moonlight
walk when he had seen Mrs. Whitman,
instantly his "Helen of Helens," behind
the red house in its snug garden, her hand
athwart the single rose she was cutting,
the sudden turn she made, her vanishing
into the cellar door whose soundless closing
stopped his breathing, as though to profane

this vision with any sound were unthinkable.
"I've sent her the poem with my recollection,"
he tells Pabodie, and shows him a copy.
Pabodie reads it and says: "Ah. lovely! A blank verse
paean to our finest poet. Her eyes — what lines! —
two sweetly scintilant Venuses! She will fall
into your power, rest assured, Mr. Poe."

"There was more to the poem," Poe confided,
"but I ought not frighten this Helen of Helens
with the thought of an apparition I saw,
or thought I saw —"

                    "An *apparition*?"
up went one of Pabodie's black eyebrows.
"You know their garden wall drops down
to the Episcopal churchyard, do you not?"

<226>

"I did not note it then."

                              "Tell what you saw,
and I will say if it has some common thread
with what *some* have said about that hillside
and what transpires at night there."

Poe turned over his manuscript, half-read
and half-invented as he spoke memory:
"But stay, pale Prophetess! Hold back the moon
And those hoarded clouds that would conceal it!
Return and calm my frensied observing
Of a glowing form that rises — a form
I thought dead, that sleeps no more — it mounts
To speak its dread name into my hearing.
It spoke — not words in any human tongue! —
Thank God it did not speak *that name* or mine! —
A kind of half-whistled ululation.
Its eyes, two darkly luminous nebulae,
Caught mine, and sparked, and spurned me.
Then, folding in its shroud-like trail, it leaped
With superhuman will to the trellis,
Up, up, vertiginous, three storeys up
And either to roof or into attic
It vanished: all this in my one heartbeat,
In the darkness of one cloud's passing."

"What did you make of it?" asked Pabodie.
"You do not strike me, Poe, as a 'ghost' man."

"Ghosts, no! Place emanations, if you will,
or astral doubles our souls send out and just
as easily call back. Call them *wish forms*,
mesmeric force , all manner of ill-will,:
there are many things in the universe,
and things we call to a semblance of life
by dreaming them or giving name." He paused.

<227>

"I fear the wine speaks now. Perhaps I say
too much and you think me but a madman.
I have made enemies with my science."

Pabodie smiled, and with a deft hand replaced
Poe's empty glass with its brim-full brother.
"What you have spoken of, we know quite well.
There are secrets we keep, and those we tell
because they amuse us and harm no one.
A spectre is haunting St. John's Churchyard.
Ask any of these gentlemen here — ask
and you shall hear the same tale from all."
Here Pabodie elbowed a young lawyer,
ushered him close to Poe for the telling:

"Sir, I could not but overhear. No lies
pass muster in this establishment, where friends
console and drink from sundown to midnight.
St. John's *is* haunted. I'll not be found there
on North Main on a moonless night; I'll not
look down there from Benefit Street above
if there's even a shadow in the place.

Just as you said, she comes in her own shroud,
hangs like a harpy in a spreading beech,
or spreads her tresses on a tabletop grave,
or darts from fence to yew to tombstone.

A harmless fairy, the sexton tells us
(but rum-full he sleeps, and never sees her).
They say her eyes can catch you, and once caught
you are lured to pass the night there, amid
the worms and moss and broken markers,
and if her eyes catch you, your life is hers

<228>

sunset in providence

to do with as she pleases Night after night
she'll have you there for her pleasure, your pain.
Point out some wreck of a man in an alley
and all will say: 'Lucy has ruined him.'"

"Lucy?" Poe asked. "Why, of all names, Lucy?"

"That's what she calls herself. Sometimes she speaks
her name or a few lines of poetry."

Here Pabodie broke in, "And then she's gone,
as thin as smoke and pale as a firefly."

"So I have seen a spectre — the very same?"

"So, Mr. Poe, it would seem. I counsel you
to keep to yourself your summer vision.
The families on Benefit, you see,
have secrets, and keep them. Monsieur Dupin
would be hard-pressed to decipher them all."

<229>

Here Pabodie would say no more, but one
far voice from a distant table called out,
as an old sailor made bid to join them:

"Aye, that's *Saucy Lucy* y'er speakin o'.
She ain't no spirit, unless that 'spectre' word
is your gentleman's way of sayin' what
we all do see and know too well. Dark nights
she haunts the St. John's graveyard sure enough,
and if she catch your eye, an' it be late
and the sexton be well into slumber,
then many's the man that'ud go to her.
And as for doin' her biddin', that ain't
supernatural since she be wantin'
pretty much what the sailors be wantin'."

Pabodie paled and, finding a handkerchief,
shielded himself from the sailor's breath.
"I don't give credit to these bawdy tales,"
he said to Poe. "They hear — perhaps they see —
and to cover their fear they *embellish*."

Poe nodded. "For a gentleman, a ghost
suffices, a lonely ghost beyond all hope,
ephemeral, untouchable, some virgin
ripped from her life by contagion."
Poe stopped, choked, put out the glass
for another turn from the wine-cask.

<230>

II.
Past-midnight, Providence was wide awake.
"The Raven" was requested, recited.
Then arm in arm he walked with Pabodie
to a Chinese laundry's doorway; from there,
having passed a yellow paper beneath it,
and waiting a seeming eternity,
the two poets entered a passageway
far into the hillside, into a damp room,
a ratty, fungoid, wet-walled warren
where a dozen reclining sleepers lay,
and beside them a dozen expiring pipes,
and Poe consented to stay.

When that was done, when dreams
beyond Coleridge, of galaxies borne
on a cosmic wind, of worlds created
from mere thoughts, and as readily destroyed
convinced him of his godhood, and madness —
and that was quite enough of that, he fled.

Alone as ever, and having walked
Mr. Pabodie to his High Street home,
Poe did what it was Poe's nature to do:
at every moment the most awful thing
he could think of. He stood, at last,
at the foot of St. John's churchyard.

And there were sounds, and with raven hair and
night-dark great-coat he passed for shadow
within shadow as he climbed the hill,
and he saw them, and what they were doing.
And the man fled. And the shrouded spectre
rose up from a cold lime table marker
and her white shroud billowed around her
and parted so she was full upon him
in her nakedness, a *lamia*, her eyes afire —
he felt her will like a maelstrom, insatiable,

<231>

unquenchable, to fall into her arms
like the nine-day fall into Hell, or the careen
into an empty grave. Her lips touched hot —
nails raked his neck — and Poe swooned dead away.

It was dawn when he awakened. In horror
he reached for his clothes about him
and found everything in place. His head
seemed under a great bell, his tongue
as stiff as an iron clapper, the taste
of rust, of iron, in his mouth; he wiped
and found blood there. He looked about
and found no footprints on the damp earth
save those of his own zigzag ascent.
With Dupin's eye he surveyed all: the street
below, where one slow wagon was passing,
pulled by a somnolent mare; the high street
above the churchyard, seen only in gaps
between the garden walls and houses.
Only the shrubs and trees, and the darkness
of certain nights made this a private place.
His perverse imp had brought him here. And what
of the spectre? Did she hang even now
from some rooftop, or sleep beneath the lid
of a vaulted gravestone? No answers here,
but what was *this*? Poe strode to a gravestone
and found upon it a splendid binding,
a finely-printed edition of a book he knew,

"By the author of the Waverly novels" —
The Bride of Lammermoor. Lucy Ashton
is its doomed heroine: her first love lost,
she kills her bridegroom on her wedding night.
On the end leaf was an inscription, rubbed
out by an angry hand, and "S –A –P."

<232>

III.
"My mother, Mrs. Power." Poe bowed;
perhaps he bowed too deeply, perhaps
the bead-line of nervous moisture
across his brow betrayed him. He smelled,
not Muddy's faint rose, but camphor,
mildew and dampened woolens.
"We are honored to receive you, sir,"
the widow Power said stiffly.
"The honor is mine," Poe smiled, eyes lit
with the importuning son's mother-plea,
and she seemed to soften. He had not slipped.

Now Helen, her scarves aflutter, turned,
as another woman swept down the stairs
and into the dim-lit parlor. His hosts
seem startled. "My sister," spoke Helen,
"Miss Susan Anna Power." Poe bowed
as the slight figure, indifferently coiffed
and double-layered with a Chinese robe
thrown over a haze of many-layered skirts,
burst between Helen and her mother.
Poe bowed again. But silently, an awkward
suitor's pause on seeing a younger sister,
to outward view, an appropriate
deference to an unmarried woman,
but his inner voice spelled out:
Susan — **A**nna — **P**ower.

"The Raven has come to roost!" said Susan.
"The Raven comes to seize the dove —" The frowns
of Mrs. Power, and Helen's consternation,
were what they *thought* caused her to pause.
But no, she *spied the book* in Poe's left hand
against his charcoal-colored overcoat,

<233>

and flying across the parlor to him, as though
in salutation, half-bow, half-curtsey, she seized
the marble-edged volume, nails pressed
into the oak-brown leather with uncommon force.
She spoke in a sepulchral voice, so low
as to seem baritone, and from a distance:
"When the last Laird of Ravenswood
    to Ravenswood shall ride —"
To which Poe declined his head and answered:
"And woo a dead maiden to be his bride."
She parried "He shall stable his steed in the Kelpie's flow."
He ended, "And his name shall be lost for evermoe!"
And deftly, *The Bride of Lammermoor* passed
before the uncomprehending eyes
of the wooed one and the watchful mother.
And deftly, *The Bride of Lammermoor* passed
to *The Succubus of St. John's Churchyard*!

<234>

THE TREE AT LOVECRAFT'S GRAVE

This solemn spreading beech
was once a perfect hemisphere
of waxy red-green foliage.
Now it is crippled and sere,
scarred by the pruning
   of diseased limbs,
trunk bared, a twisted bole
in the form of a petrified heart.
Its gnarled roots rake earth
with a death-row desperation.
Within another hollowed bole,
   (eye-socket for a Cyclops)
malignant mushrooms proliferate,
caps and stalks angled sunward.
The schoolboy gashes
   where fans have carved initials
   (their own and HPL's)
widen and blacken,
the once-proud limbs
   tattooed with NECRONOMICON,
   HOWARD P. LOVECRAFT '99,
   even a whole sentence
      about the primacy of fear,
runes ruinous to a living monument.

Still, the furry beech-nuts fall like hail
   to the delight of squirrels.
Still, the hard brown kernels issue forth,
each a perfect blueprint
   of a perfect tree —

or have the roots, tasting the calcium
of author's bones, the humus rot
of eye and brain and memory
mutated the germ and flower anew

<235>

so that these seeds transcend
   to sentience?

Gather these nuts, then,
   and harvest them.
First they must hibernate
   for the beech remembers glaciers.
Then they will germinate,
   pale tentacles in search
   of anchorage,
until the red-green engine
of stalk and leaf
is ready to catapult
into the sun-chase.

Will these trees move
   of their own accord?
Will their root-claws crave blood
   and the iron-rich earth
   of a crumbling grave?
Will the branches sway
   on windless nights?
Will fox-fires and will o' wisps
   paint impossible colors
on bud-ends and blossoms?
Will beech nuts burst
   to pale blue eyes
insomniac astronomers
with perfect vision,
counting the Pleaides,
numbering the galaxies.

And will they speak
   the patient sonnets
of their greater lifespans,
the long-arced lines
   their waving branches beat?

<236>

And somewhere within them,
    does *he* smile there,
transmuted poet and dreamer
subsumed into the eons?

Are those *his* thoughts
that make them tremble
    at every sunset,
his elder gods they fear
might swallow the sun
as it tosses in darkness?

Is he lord of their nightmares,
giving them Dread,
the obverse of the coin of Joy,
Fear, the companion of Wonder?

I regard the ailing tree,
    the modest gravestone.
The tree will die. The rain
    will wipe the letters clean.
Only the whispered words,
    the lines the fingers trace
from one yellowed book
    to another
endure —

I hold the burst nuts in one hand,
    a book of Lovecraft's tales in the other.
I study the cloudless, blue, deceptive sky,
the lie that conceals an infinity
    of screaming stars —

Oh, these roots have read him,
    they have read him.

<237>

HERE AT THE POINT

Secret transcript of a meeting of The Security Committee of
Swan Point Cemetery

Here at the Point
we tolerate no nonsense.
Let the word go out
to the security guards:

photographing the monuments
is not permitted,
especially at Lovecraft's grave.

Families spend thousands
to put these obelisks and stones,
statues and mausoleums
onto our grounds

to be seen here.
Here! not in some smelly
newspaper!

If artists show up
with paints and easels,
they can depict the foliage,
but not the monuments,
not the monuments!

Use your judgment, men.
If one of those Art Club Ladies
sets up to paint, just shoo
her off politely.

But if it's a RISD kid —
one of those green-haired,
snot-nosed spray painters
from the Design School,

<238>

a little ride over
to the *trespasser's shed*
might be in order.

TV crews
are absolutely prohibited —
escort them right back
to the outer gates.

As always, no picnicking!
No food or drink
whatsoever — last month
we had a whole family
eating at a graveside
(damn Armenians!).
We stopped that in a hurry.

You can't let up,
not for a moment.
Watch for those kids,
keep an eye peeled
for lurkers, and *couples*.

Matthewson here keeps a graph
of how many conundrums
we find, and where —

conundrums, you know,
those little rubber things —
disgusting!

This is a place of repose.
Repose. Why don't they get it?
No eating, no drinking,
no urinating, no fornicating,
no congregating.

<239>

Those Lovecraft fans
are the worst. Reading their poetry,
mouthing what rituals
we can only imagine —
what the hell is *Cthulhu fhthagn*, anyway?
That Rutherford person
and those evil twins
dressed up as Lovecraft
or monks or ravens —
they have to be stopped!
Why doesn't someone stop them?

And look at their clothes,
a mockery of the good clergy
with all that black — one man
was carrying a skull! Boys with black
fingernails, Jesus! Some of the women
may not even be women.
Just imagine what they do afterward!

This Halloween, we'll stop them.
We know they're dying
to get in here at night.
Gamwell, here,
will man the portable generator.
The flood lights are set up.
The Lovecraft plot
will be as bright as day.
Just let them try to come here naked,
bringing some animal, no doubt,
to sacrifice. Not on my watch!

You, Roby, you'll get
the use of the night goggles.
Anything bigger than a badger
moves, and you'll see it.
Blair and Potter, third shift

<240>

for the two of you,
and no sleeping! I want
to see those headlights everywhere.

Next year I'll ask the trustees
to approve a guard tower
with moveable searchlights,
but I doubt they'll find the money.
What else can we do?
The ghouls are everywhere.
We just want peace and quiet.
This is a proper cemetery
and my motto has always been
As below, so above.

<241>

TO THE ARC OF THE SUBLIME

In nights beneath the stars,
    sometimes alone — sometimes
    with one I loved
        (in futile or secret urgency) —
I have outwaited
    the rise and fall of Scorpio,
        arc of its tail
            stinging the treetops.
I have traced the inconstant moon,
    the indecisive Venus;
    feel more assured
by the long, slow haul of Jupiter,
the patient tread of Pluto
    (whom they pursue
        in their frigid outer orbits
I cannot guess)

Such solitude,
    millennia between
        the fly-bys of comets,
perhaps is why
    they need so many moons,
why rings of ice
    encircle them like loyal cats.

It is lonely in space,
    far out
where the sun is merely
    a star among stars.

It is lonely in autumn.
    I sit in midnight woods.
A trio of raccoons, foraging,
    come up to me,

<242>

black mask eyes of the young ones
interrogating the first cold night,
    the unaccustomed noisiness
        of bone rattle maple leaf
           beneath their paws.
How can I tell them
    these trees will soon be skeletons,
    the pond as hard as glass,
    the nut and berry harvest over?
These two are young —
    they would not believe me.
Their mother rears up protectively,
    smells me,   scents out
    the panic among the saplings,
    the smell of rust and tannin.

We share a long stillness,
    a moment when consciousness
    is not a passive agency.

Our sight invades the countryside,
    embracing everything —
    sleepers in beds in a concrete tower —
    earthworms entwining in humus rot —
goes up and out through the limpid sky,
    streaming past moon —
        — moon's lava'd seas —
out, out, to the arc of the sublime,
    tracing the edge of great Antares,
leaping to other galaxies unafraid.

(Let space expand as though the worlds
    still feared their neighbors!
Let miser stars implode,
    their dwarf hearts shriveling
        to cores of iron!)

<243>

We are the scourge of entropy.
   We sing the one great note
      through which new being
         comes out of nothingness.

Does it have meaning,
   this seed-shagged planet
      alive with eyes?
Is earth the crucible,
   sandbox of angry gods,
or is it the eye of all eyes,

   ear of all ears,
the nerve through which the universe
   acquires self-knowledge?

But these are weighty thoughts
   for man and mammal!
We are but blood and minerals,
   upright for an instant,
   conscious for but a moment,
   a grain-fall of cosmic hourglass.
Yet I am not ephemeral:
   I freeze time,
      relive moments
         chronicle the centuries
      re-speak Shakespeare,
         beat out the staves of Mozart,
           read the same books
           my forebears knew
         make of old words
           my wordy pyramid.
I am the one
   snapping the pictures of solar systems,
   sending myself
      an outside-in self-portrait.
I send my name and signature
   on bottles spinning past Uranus.

<244>

I am the one who asks, Is it worth it?
I who hear the X-ray wind reply, It is!

I am the one who would not stay in caves,
    I was discontent in the treetops.
I wanted to be bird and whale and rocket.

Ever, o ever more mortal now —
    — friends falling away like withered leaves —
still I find joy in this subliminal shrine of autumn.
My hand is full of fossil shells
    picked up from the lake shore rubble,
scallops enduring with the same rock faith
    (implicit minimum vocabulary):
I live, and the increase of my consciousness
                is the span of my life.

<245>

ABOUT THE POEMS

The following notes provide a few words about most of the poems in this book. These are things a reader might wish to know by way of background. Only a handful of these poems require narrow or special knowledge; they are "occasional" pieces and I note them accordingly.

OCTOBER IS COMING is the anthem of my emigration to New England in 1985. It was written in Providence on the day I decided to pack up my New York belongings — the accretion of some 16 years — and relocate. Its language suggests that old New England transcendentalism has long been part of my nature.

THE STATE VERSUS AUTUMN is a satire on law-and-order fanatics, censors and bureaucrats. It mocks the numskulls who perceive Satanic plots in every artistic expression that touches upon the dark, magical, or here, even autumnal. Although the success of *Harry Potter* and *Twilight* and *Buffy, The Vampire Slayer* and other pop-culture Gothics is a real ascendancy for the dark and creepy, the desire to stifle the supernatural is still out there.

THE SAILOR AND THE OAK NYMPHS incorporates the three wood nymphs the ancient Greeks associated with the oak tree: Amaltheia the virgin, Io the nymph, and the crone Adrasteia. See Robert Graves' *The Greek Myths*.

END OF THE WORLD is a new twist on the falling leaves theme. It describes what happens when gravity becomes selective and the earth sheds its people into space. It was probably written after seeing a couple of bizarre Christian comic books about the Rapture. The failure of the Rapture to arrive after repeated announcements of its coming does not deter the criminal minds of the preachers who persuade their followers to part with all their worldly goods in preparation for the end of the world. The last Rapture preacher in 2011 had amassed something like $17 million from his followers.

I have a counterproposal: send *me* money, and I guarantee I will *stop* the Rapture from happening.

THE OUTSIDER is one of my most personal poems, and was, at the time this book was published, the apex of *Anniversarius*, my autumn poem cycle. It sums up how one can be an outsider to the common life others lead — and enjoy it. There are many ironies and tensions in assuming the Outsider role and this poem tries to explore them.

<247>

SON OF DRACULA recalls my childhood fascination with vampires. There was a year when I even wished to become a vampire. I wore a black cape, learned how to hypnotize people, and left the window open at night hoping for bats. I still cringe when I see a cross. The first version of this poem was merely descriptive and suggestive; in the revision I have explored the "outsider" aspect of my young vampire fantasies, which occurred just as I was discovering poetry. In the fall of 2010 I revisited Scottdale, PA and saw the books (if not the actual, long-gone library). I was gratified to see a brand-new library facing an attractive little park and gazebo.

The "hated town" referred to in the poem is not Scottdale, my childhood home, but West Newton, the town where my mother and evil stepfather took me for the rest of my high school years. The profound misery of family life there colors the poem; the people there treated me kindly, considering what a demented teenager I was, vampire cape and all.

THE ARGUMENT is based on a visit to Longfellow's grave in Mt Auburn Cemetery, Cambridge, MA. Shortly after the visit I learned of Longfellow's and Emerson's unkind remarks about Poe.

AVOIDING THE MUSE reflects on my feelings after I returned to writing poems after a hiatus. During the period when I wrote two novels there was no poetry in sight.

ASHES AND EQUINOX, MARS IN CONJUNCTION is an elegy written the day of the death of poet Barbara Holland. We were friends for many years and created many companion poems which we read together in New York. This poem refers to the strange *omens* of the day, mentioned in the footnote. There are allusions here to a number of Barbara's poems and themes. Those who do not know her work will, I fear, miss many allusions, but I hope the poem nevertheless has some more universal appeal. We lost a great voice when Barbara left us.

WRITER'S BLOCK was written for Barbara A. Holland after she described a two-year hiatus in her own writing. By turning the psychological barrier into a huge slab of stone, I also evoke the world of petrified objects so often shown in Magritte paintings. Barbara and I both used Magritte images as take-off points for poems, so I am writing here in the manner of her great cycle, *Crises of Rejuvenation*.

BOARD GAME is about being infatuated — and being pursued. It sums up one of life's tragic ironies: the unlikelihood of mutual attraction.

CREATION REVISITED is a jest, based upon a curious discovery I made when studying the supposed calendar of creation. As my readers know, I never use Hebrew or Christian mythology except to make fun of human folly. The Lovecraftian monster in the poem is prophetic of The Giant Flying Spaghetti Monster (GFSM), a wonderful religious hoax.

<248>

DEER HUNTERS was inspired by a trip to North Adams in the Berkshires and an overnight stay in a hotel full of deer hunters. The idea of the hunters freezing in the forest while the deer lived it up in the hotel was a delicious one.

EDGAR AND HELEN is based *partially* on the actual failed romance of Edgar Allan Poe and Providence poet Sarah Helen Whitman. Shortly before the planned marriage, Sarah Helen assigned her personal fortune to her mother. Poe then broke an alcoholic temperance vow, perhaps on purpose, then took an overdose of laudanum whose aftermath was the breaking off of the engagement. The dialogue of Poe and Helen is imaginary and convoluted: I make fun of the flowery way in which two literary figures might have conversed. The fantasy at the end of the poem in which Poe imagines using all the tortures from his own stories on Helen and her family leads to an intimation of his own death, less than one year later. The poem is also based *partially* on a doomed Providence romance of my own, and its inaccuracies involve introducing equally convoluted torments of my own; hence, there are no *actual* quotations from Poe or Mrs. Whitman. In the years since I wrote this poem, I find myself reading, or reciting in front of Mrs, Whitman's house, the last stanzas of this poem. I don't think I've ever read the whole poem aloud: a thing for the page and not the ear. I have since written an entire book about the Poe/Helen romance: *Last Flowers: The Romance and Poetry of Edgar Allan Poe and Sarah Helen Whitman*, and a fantasy poem about Poe, Helen, and her insane sister, found in the Appendix to this volume.

VISA GRANTED, WITH GRAVEL is based on a news account from 1986 of a young man who burst through Checkpoint Charlie in a truck full of gravel. Shortly thereafter, one of the border guards at that checkpoint — perhaps even one who shot at the escaping truck — also fled to the West, provoking the companion poem BORDER GUARD. The latter poem appeared in the libertarian journal *Liberty* just months before the Berlin Wall began to crumble. I have never been more elated to have two poems become "obsolete." (Ah, but the lessons of history are never obsolete.)

SIDEWAYS IN PASSING will ring a bell for anyone who has ever had an obsessive infatuation followed by "a pact of mutual avoidance."

VALKYRIES ON ROUTE 128 puts those beautiful German maidens who carried off the bodies of heroes from the battlefield onto today's *real* slaughter ground: the highway.

IVAN GROZNI is Russian for Ivan the Terrible. This was the nickname given to a Cleveland auto worker, John Demianiuk, who was uncovered as a dreaded prison guard at Treblinka. After three deportation trials in the United States he was sent to Israel for trial, where he was found guilty of being "The Beast of Treblinka." He was later freed on appeal and returned to the United States. Further trials resulted in his deportation,

<249>

and, finally, another trial in Germany. He was finally convicted of war crimes.

SPARE CHANGE is about a perennial derelict on Providence's East Side, who for some reason picked the windiest spot in town as his hangout. He vanished shortly after this book was published.

MILL TOWNS is a reflection on the sad old factory buildings that I see along the tracks when I ride from Providence to New York on the train.

PLAGUE gives a little of their own medicine to priests and demagogues who perpetuate the insane cult of sex-as-sin and disease-as-retribution. It also reflects the plague paranoia that accompanied the early years of the AIDS crisis.

JUST REWARDS is a prose poem making fun of armchair Marxists, by showing what would happen if Heaven itself became a People's State in a Maoist mode. A lot of people who had elaborate blueprints on how to re-engineer society never had to live in a workers' paradise. It gave me a chance to go after both Christianity and Marxist hokum at the same time. If language, as Richard Dawkins suggests, is the software of the human genome, both of these belief systems are bad software.

THE EVANGELICALS ARE COMING! is another diatribe. It was written during the presidential candidacy of the religious con man Pat Robertson, but its point is still worth making. Since there is no bottom to human gullibility, there is no end of con artists. I originally titled the poem, "The Christians Are Coming," but I'll back off on that. I've known some nice Unitarians and Quakers.

BLUMENSTÜCKE is German for "Flower Piece," a title used for several 19th Century piano works. The poem is a satire on sexual repression, countering the proper conversation of a minister and some spinsters with the unsuspected orgy of bees and flowers around them. After all, flowers are the sexual parts of plants and Puritans should be shocked to know what's happening in the nearest vase.

ROADSIDE VIEWS is another poem written on the train to and from New York. Related, but in a very different vein, is a "get even" poem called RUINS, which uses an extended metaphor of a ruined factory for the once-loved one.

WATER SPRITE was inspired by a midnight bicycle ride along the Seekonk in Providence, and the appearance — and disappearance — of a nude figure alongside a lagoon.

THE GOD'S EYE: A SUMMER DIARY is a cycle of poems written during a summer of travel to Pennsylvania, upstate New York, and the woods of New Jersey. The opening poem, BLUEBERRIES, introduces the berry image that will link all the other poems, as well as the image of the God's Eye, a Native American symbol that consists of multicolored strings wound diagonally around a cross.

<250>

INDIAN ROCK SHELTER recounts an evening of camping near the Wanaque Reservoir in New Jersey, and a vision of the Indians who once shared the same spot. These rock shelters were in continuous use for thousands of years.

In AT THE COKE OVENS I revisit the site of my childhood home, Carpentertown, PA, and find it a blasted heath of coal dust and blackberries.

THE CEMETERY BY THE LAKE is one of many poems using a pioneers' graveyard in the village of Edinboro, Pennsylvania. Whenever I return to this, my college town, I am compelled to use the haunted spot for another poem. The lake was the site of winter festivals for the extinct Erie Indians. I had a vision of what they might have done on these waters, and for realism I added some ceremonial lines from the Onondaga dialect. The lines are real but my recreation of Erie ritual is purely imaginary. I had already translated the openings verses of the Iroquois Funeral Rites, "At the Wood's Edge," but I found nothing there that directly provoked the contents of this imagined ritual.

ARIADNE was abandoned on an island by Theseus, but better things were in store for her: she was rescued by Bacchus. In the tradition of Baroque cantatas and operas, I have written several "scenas" around powerful or abandoned women: Ariadne, Queen Jocasta, and Empress Carlota of Mexico.

REMEMBERING MEDEA portrays the fallen hero Jason after his wife Medea has used witchcraft to kill the King of Corinth and the king's daughter, and then murdered her own children — all in revenge for Jason's plan to abandon her and marry the princess. Now Jason, a reviled outcast, sits by the shore and remembers what it was like to be married to the powerful witch.

FRAGMENTS OF A HYMN TO RHEA, THE OAK TREE GODDESS is for pagans and Greek myth specialists. Drawn to the Chthonic and primal myths, I tried to include everything that is known about the oak goddess into one poem. It is also an experiment in alternating long lines with two-part lines with a caesura. This was done to convey, via old English tradition, a sense of ritual and antiquity. This is a poetic merging, then, of the world of Odin with that of the Olympians.

GANYMEDE is a modern elaboration of a unique rape and transformation myth in Greek mythology. Ganymede, a teenaged boy, is carried off by Zeus. Zeus's *female* abductees always came to an unhappy end, either killed by Hera or transformed into shrubs, flowers, animals or constellations to protect them from jealous Hera's wrath. Ovid devotes only two stanzas in the *Metamorphoses* to the Ganymede myth, not out of any prudery, but because the Ganymede story has a happy ending. The boy becomes the favored cup-bearer of the gods and for all we know is still

<251>

there on Olympus. It struck me that the story could be retold as a modern poem on human diversity and as a study in the concept of tolerance.

One thing led to another, and the story continued. THE RANSOM OF GANYMEDE portrays the efforts of Ganymede's father to discover the whereabouts of his son. Since Ganymede's father is the first King of Troy, and hence the forebear of Rome, the gods have a lot to say to him. I did not intend to write a prequel to *The Iliad* when I started out, but this is how it has evolved.

In HERA AND GANYMEDE, I complete the cycle, in which Hera lets down her hair and talks about sex among the gods. Finally, she comes to accept Zeus's bisexual nature and a new harmony prevails in the Heavens. Even Gods cannot help whom they love, she admits, because "Beauty's a god the mere gods worship." If only it were so on earth.

The Ganymede poems have provoked strong reactions. When the first part was published in *The Brown Classical Journal*, a student editor felt compelled to omit the love scenes, which I had carefully crafted. He also rewrote a number of lines and added things of his own devising, none of which I knew of until the poem was in print.

I smile to recall one friend, a college teacher, admonishing me not to write about this subject matter. I have yet to be picketed and my house has not yet been surrounded by a vigil of praying nuns. It has probably not occurred to the censors that this cycle of poems is the *Lolita* of Greek myth. I've been spared, I suppose, because no one takes poetry seriously enough to be threatened by it, and Bible-thumpers can't even *pronounce* Ganymede.

The cycle, THINGS SEEN IN GRAVEYARDS presents a sampling of the odd things I have seen and experienced in cemeteries around the country. The poems are self-explanatory. When read as a group they are a suite, ranging from whimsical to terrifying to transcendental. (More poems in this grouping ensued, and they are now in their own collection, *Things Seen From Graveyards*.)

The last poem included here, THE SWAN POINT GHOUL, was written two months after the ceremonies honoring the 50th anniversary of the death of horror writer H.P. Lovecraft. I went back and discovered that the grave on which I had stood had collapsed, leading to this grisly speculation.

I owe a debt to Shirley Powell for her poem about people who steal country tombstones as conversation pieces. Her poem provoked me to write THE McWILLIAMS' COFFEE TABLE, a satire about keeping up with the Joneses.

<252>

SCENES FROM A MEXICAN VAMPIRE MOVIE came from an elaborate dream from which I woke up laughing. I dashed to the computer and this humorous fantasy resulted. The poem has been adapted as a comic and is one of my most popular pieces at live readings.

I lost my companion of 16 years, Thunderpuss the Cat, a temperamental lilac Siamese. The poem VIGIL combines my feelings about the imminent demise of the cat, along with my admiration for the noble philosophy of the Roman poet Lucretius. The long poem, THUNDERPUSS: IN MEMORIAM, is my tribute and farewell. If you do not like cats, skip this one. At readings, this is a three-hanky poem.

LOW TIDE is based upon a dream related by Providence's native son, the horror writer H.P. Lovecraft. The poem is an expansion and retelling of his dream.

AT LOVECRAFT'S GRAVE is a memorial poem honoring the personality, spirit and writing of H.P. Lovecraft (1890-1937), who is now regarded as the greatest American horror writer since Poe. I was present at the 50th Anniversary rites, and wrote this poem immediately afterwards. It has since been read at the grave site annually and has been widely circulated among Lovecraftians. Like all such poems, it has allusions to the subject's biography and writings. I cannot elaborate them here. Although this is a poem for specialists, it contains some material that I regard as universal. Most particular is my defense of the supernatural in literature: "...our secret of secrets, how we are the gentle ones, how terror is our tightrope over life, how we alone can comprehend the smile behind the skull."

Although this volume was published as a showcase of all the new poetry I wrote during my early years in Providence, the occasion of a second edition permits me to add, as an appendix, these last six additional poems that use Providence or Rhode Island as locale.

MIDNIGHT ON BENEFIT STREET, 1935 describes the town's most famous street as Lovecraft would have known it in his last decade of life. There are references to the mummy and the Buddha in the Rhode Island School of Design Museum, the now-closed tunnel connecting downtown to the Seekonk river, the Athenaeum library, and the Brown family mansion.

OCTOBER THOUGHTS IN WAR-TIME describe a walk past the Unitarian Church on Benefit Street.

LUCY: A MYSTERY, uses accurate details from the Poe-Mrs. Whitman romance and from them, speculates about the madness of Mrs. Whitman's sister. It also provides a tantalizing link between Poe and Sir Walter Scott.

<253>

THE TREE AT LOVECRAFT'S GRAVE has become one of my most popular poems. After the management of Swan Point Cemetery demanded apologies for the insult to their tree and forbade photography at the Lovecraft gravesite, I sent a secret agent to attend a meeting of the cemetery's security department, the transcript of which can be read here in HERE AT THE POINT.

In a more serious and poetic vein, TO THE ARC OF THE SUBLIME was written on the banks of the Seekonk River.

<254>

ABOUT THE POET

Brett Rutherford, born in Scottdale, Pennsylvania, began writing poetry seriously during a stay in San Francisco. During his college years at Edinboro State College (now Edinboro University) in Pennsylvania, he published an underground newspaper and printed his first hand-made poetry chapbook. He moved to New York City, where he founded The Poet's Press in 1971. For more than 20 years, he worked as an editor, journalist, printer, and consultant to publishers and nonprofit organizations.

After a literary pilgrimage to Providence, Rhode Island, on the track of H.P. Lovecraft and Edgar Allan Poe, he moved there with his press. *Poems From Providence* was the fruit of his first three years in the city (1985-1988), published in 1991. Since then, he has written a study of Edgar Allan Poe and Providence poet Sarah Helen Whitman (briefly Poe's fiancee), a biographical play about Lovecraft, and his second novel, *The Lost Children* (Zebra Books, 1988). The various themes shown in *Poems From Providence* have since yielded separate volumes: *Things Seen in Graveyards* (2007), *Anniversarius: The Autumn Poems* (1984, 1996), and *Twilight of the Dictators* (1992, 2009). Further collected poems appear in *The Gods As They Are, On their Planets* (2005), *Whippoorwill Road: The Supernatural Poems* (1998, 2005), *An Expectation of Presences* (2011). *Trilobite Love Song* (2014) and *The Pumpkined Heart: The Pennsylvania Poems* (2017).

Returning to school for a master's degree in English, Rutherford completed this project in 2007, and now works for University of Rhode Island in distance learning, and teaches for the Women's Studies Department. There, he has created courses on "The Diva," "Women in Science Fiction," and "Radical American Women." He has prepared annotated editions of Matthew Gregory Lewis's *Tales of Wonder*, the poetry of Charles Hamilton Sorley, A.T. Fitzroy's antiwar novel *Despised and Rejected*, and the first volume of the collected writings of Emilie Glen. The poet returned to his native Pennsylvania in 2015, taking up residence in the Squirrel Hill neighborhood of Pittsburgh.

His interests include classical music and opera; Chinese art, history and literature; bicycling, graveyards, woods, horror films, intellectual history, and crimes against nature.

<255>

ABOUT THE ILLUSTRATOR

Pieter Vanderbeck was born in Rochester, NY in 1944, and began drawing and writing in grade school (when he decided that would be his destiny). In 1960 he moved to Providence and studied painting at the Rhode Island School of Design. With a large series of poems and drawings in 1964, he began his lifework proper, and since has done thousands of either. His preferred drawing medium is the Rapidograph pen, a choice influenced by the etchings of Matisse and the woodcuts of Utamaro. Other artists to influence his work are Bosch, Goya and Klee. Both his drawings and paintings are built chiefly on music, most notably Schubert, Bruckner and Shostakovich. He draws inferences from oblique cross references, being a committed eclecticist. He hopes to live to complete Opus 50000.

Vanderbeck retired after many years on the staff of the Rhode Island School of Design Museum. He spends several months each year drawing in the Adirondacks.

<256>

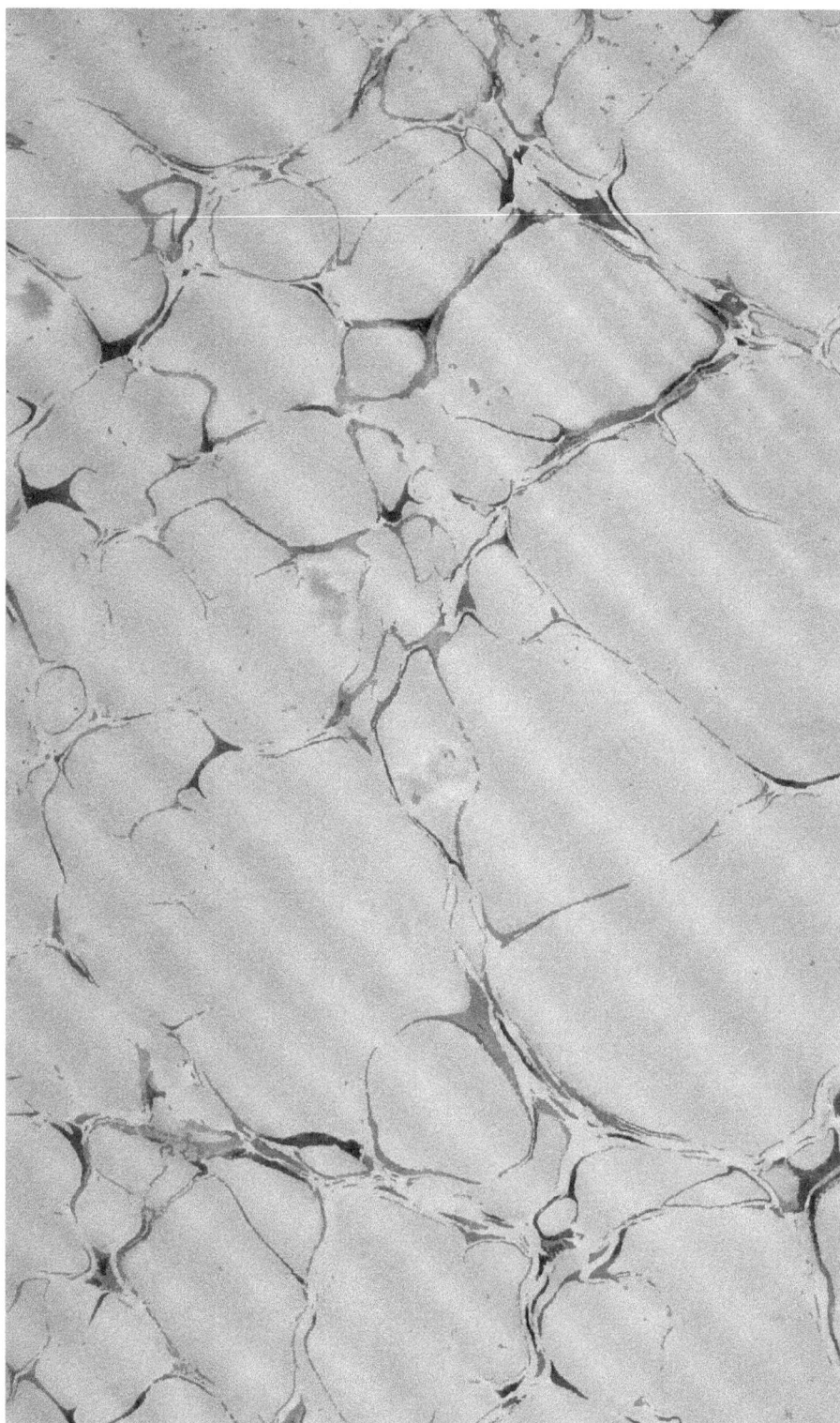

www.ingramcontent.com/pod-product-compliance
Lightning Source LLC
Chambersburg PA
CBHW021355090426
42742CB00009B/869